# ⚡ THE ⚡
# SUPERKIDS
# ACTIVITY GUIDE
## TO CONQUERING EVERY DAY

# ⚡ THE ⚡
# SUPERKIDS
# ACTIVITY GUIDE

## TO CONQUERING EVERY DAY

Awesome Games and Crafts to Master Your Moods, Boost Focus, Hack Mealtimes
and Help Grown-Ups Understand Why You Do the Things You Do

## DAYNA ABRAHAM

Award-Winning Educator and Founder of Lemon Lime Adventures

PAGE STREET
PUBLISHING CO.

To my own superkids—Legoman, Bones and Super B, who drive me to be the best grown-up sidekick I can be. Here's to many more years of honing your superpowers and conquering the world!

PAGE STREET
PUBLISHING CO.

First published in 2017 by

Page Street Publishing Co.

27 Congress Street, Suite 105

Salem, MA 01970

www.pagestreetpublishing.com

Distributed by Macmillan, sales in Canada by The Canadian Manda Group.

21  20  19  18  17   2  3  4  5

ISBN-13: 978-1-62414-415-8

ISBN-10: 1-62414-415-2

Library of Congress Control Number:  2017932263

Cover and book design by Page Street Publishing Co.

Photography by Dayna Abraham, except pages 62 and 178 by Jennifer Tammy

Template designs by Brittany Mays

Printed and bound in the United States

# TABLE OF CONTENTS

# THE SUPERKIDS MANIFESTO

We are *unique*. We embrace our differences and let them shine.

We are *adventurous*. We take risks and push ourselves to try the impossible.

We are *spirited*. We use our emotions and energy to change the world.

We are *creative*. We are constantly inventing, creating and dreaming of the unknown.

We are *fierce*. We are tough and take a stand for what we believe in.

*We are superkids.*

We aren't picky, anxious, difficult, messy or strong-willed. We are misunderstood.

From this day forward, we will be known as superkids. This is our guide to conquering every day and helping the grown-ups in our lives understand why we do the things we do!

# INTRODUCTION

Hey Superkid,

Yeah, I'm talking to you. Don't look over your shoulder and try to find the "superkid" I am talking about. It's not your neighbor, your older brother or even your best friend. Nope, I am talking to you! Go ahead and say it, so you believe it: "I am a SUPERKID."

There, didn't that feel good? Go ahead and say it one more time, just to make sure it sinks in: "I am a SUPERKID."

Before you start to think of all the reasons you can't possibly be a superkid, I want to stop you. You see, even the most famous rock stars have doubt and don't believe in themselves every day. This doesn't mean they are any less super. And even superheroes have struggles and pitfalls. That doesn't make them any less super, either. The truth is, despite your struggles, your mistakes or your bad days . . . you are a superkid! The Superkids Manifesto is yours. I want you to own it.

You are *unique*.

You are *adventurous*.

You are *spirited*.

You are *creative*.

You are *fierce*.

You are a SUPERKID.

You are going to conquer the world and I am going to help you every step of the way, starting with this book.

Now that you know I'm talking to you and you believe you are a superkid, let's get a few more things straight. Do you have a minute? I know you are super busy and have even thought about skipping over this page to get to the bright colorful activities, but I promise you, you will want to hear what I have to say!

In this book, I am going to teach you to embrace who you are and challenge you to stretch yourself in new ways.

I will teach you to:

- Recognize your likes and dislikes, understand all eight of your super senses and hone your UNIQUE set of strengths and struggles.

- Challenge your ADVENTUROUS nature through tools that encourage flexible thinking, games that push you to try new things and strategies that will break down the barriers that hold you back.

- Help your grown-ups harness all your energy, encourage positive thinking and master your SPIRITED moods through fun activities.

- Fine-tune your organizational skills, develop systems to boost your memory and create hacks to keep you focused and on task while preserving your CREATIVE brain.

- Tame your FIERCE side enough to take a stand in a respectful way, become an expert on how you process information and be a champion for yourself.

I know the world sees you as picky, anxious, difficult, messy or even strong-willed. Don't believe those labels. You are just right.

Now, it's time to dig deep, learn how you tick (why you do the things you do) and show the world the SUPERKID you already are! In fact, in this book, I am going to teach you how to flip the world's language and the way it sees you by giving you a peek into the brains of the grown-ups that love you and the science behind your behaviors.

Are you ready to own the title "SUPERKID"? Great! Now, copy that manifesto and make it yours. Put it on your wall, put it in your room or put it on your refrigerator. Wherever you put it, remember it. Say it every day. Believe it.

"I AM A SUPERKID."

I can't wait to help you unleash the superpowers you already have. You know you are a superkid. I know you are a superkid. Now, let's show the world you are a superkid. Together, we are going to conquer the world one day at a time. Are you with me?

Your superpowered friend,

*Dayna Abraham*

# HOW TO USE THIS BOOK ⚡

Before you jump into the rest of the book, I want to set the stage for you so you can get the absolute most out of every dollar you (or your grown-up) spent on this book. While this is the boring nitty-gritty stuff we have to go over, I promise I won't bore you too much. In fact, I might even make you crack a smile. One thing I promise, by the end of all these extra words, you will know exactly how to use this book as you go forward to conquer the world one day at a time.

Inside you will find 75 projects to help you be your best self, harness your rock-star attitude and boost your inner superpowers. These projects are broken down into six easy-to-digest chapters by the time of day they will be the most useful for you: mornings, mealtime, wait times, learning, playtime and nighttime.

As an example, let's say your biggest struggle comes in the mornings when you just can't seem to get yourself together to get out the door, and it seems all your adults can do is nag, nag, nag. This is the chapter you've been waiting for your whole life. Or maybe you are a very particular eater and almost dread mealtimes with other people because you know someone is going to say something about what and how you eat. Flip to the mealtime hacks and find some solutions to revolutionize your day and flip those "quit being so picky" jabs into something a little more positive.

Whatever your struggle is throughout your day, I've got you covered. By the end of this book, the world will discover you are a super listener, a super son/daughter, a super student, a super friend and most of all . . . a super YOU!

## The Stuff

As you flip through this book to find a tool that is perfect for you, you might begin to notice that many of the projects need "stuff." As kids, I know it can be hard to find the perfect material or item to make something out of an activity book, so I've tried really hard to make sure the stuff is easy to find or super inexpensive (if you have to buy it). My favorite places to gather materials are the recycling bin, my old junk drawers, the kitchen cabinets and the craft drawer. On the rare occasion you need to buy something, check out the dollar store or thrift stores before heading to your local grocery or craft store. Almost every item needed for this book can be found in one of those places.

One of the most important things to remember is that many of these materials are starting points to spark your imagination. So, don't worry if you don't have all the stuff to make a tool you really can't wait to make. Get creative and invent a new way to make your tool.

## Made Just for You

Do activities add more stress than help because they seem too hard or have too many steps? Are you already dreading some of the projects because you feel you don't have what it takes to make it look just right? Let me tell you a little secret: I'm not a fancy-shmancy crafty person either. I can't sew, I can't cut a straight line to save my life and I can't even work on a project for a long period of time without getting distracted. Does that sound familiar? You see, I made each and every one of these projects with you in mind.

Many of these activities don't even require any materials at all, like the restaurant games or the seated exercises. All you need is your body. In addition, I've made every project no-sew, no-cook and no-fail. That's right, you can't fail. In fact, I even tested the projects on my own three kids before sharing them with you, and I can assure you, you will be successful at these projects!

## Super Senses

Are you sitting down right now? Good, because I need to tell you something really important that might rock everything you thought you knew about your senses. Let's start with a little quiz. How many senses do you have? Did you guess five? In a way, you are right, but not completely. Sight, hearing, touch, taste and smell are the ones you've probably already been taught in school. However, those aren't your only senses.

In fact, you have many, many senses that your body uses every single day. For the purpose of this book, we are going to talk about your eight super senses and how they directly connect to your success on a day-to-day basis:

- Visual (say: vizh-oo-uhl) sense of **sight**
- Olfactory (say: ol-fak-tuh-ree) sense of **smell**
- Auditory (say: aw-di-tawr-ee) sense of **hearing**
- Gustatory (say: guhs-tuh-tawr-ee) sense of **taste**
- Tactile (say: tak-til) sense of **touch**

- Proprioceptive (say: proh-pree-uh-sep-tiv) sense of **body awareness**
- Vestibular (say: ve-stib-yuh-ler) sense of **movement**
- Interoceptive (say: in-ter-oh-sep-tiv) sense of **internal cues**

Don't worry about memorizing these right now. We will talk a lot more about them throughout the whole book. In fact, every activity highlights the super senses you use, so you can support your senses and fine-tune your sensory preferences.

## The "Just Right" Energy Scale

Have you ever noticed that some days you feel like you could conquer the world, running from activity to activity, jumping out of your seat or even doing somersaults in the living room? Your energy seems to be bursting from your fingertips. Other times, you feel like the weight of the world is literally on your shoulders. No matter how hard you try, you can barely keep your head up, let alone get through an entire activity without leaning on the wall. This isn't your imagination playing tricks on you. The truth is, your body, brain and sensory systems are constantly changing speed.

When your body is low, you might be tired or lethargic. You might slouch, drag your feet or even be too tired to pick up a pencil. Your motivation to work is low, and your desire to conquer the world is at its lowest.

When your body is high, you might be busy or fast. You might have difficulty paying attention or sitting still, get easily agitated or have trouble listening to instructions. Your motivation to work is bypassed because you are too busy to stop and think.

However, we want our bodies to run just right. When our bodies are just right, we can attend to instructions, learn new information, wait patiently and keep our hands to ourselves. In other words, you can be a super you!

In this book, every activity has an energy scale you can use to help you reach the "just right" speed. If you are feeling like the Flash and can't sit still, look for activities lower on the energy scale to slow you down—one to three lightning bolts. On the other hand, if you are feeling more like you've been caught in your villain's webs and can't think straight, turn to activities higher on the energy scale to give you the boost you need to conquer your day—four to seven lightning bolts. On page 180 near the index, you will find a handy-dandy reference guide of all the activities in the book sorted by energy level so you can find the activity you need at the perfect moment.

## Boost Your Superpowers

Up until now, you might have thought superpowers only occurred in comic books, the movies or your favorite video games. This couldn't be further from the truth. You, my friend, are full of superpowers you don't even realize you have. My job, through this book, is to help you realize these skills and fine-tune them so you can feel successful every single day from the moment you wake up until the time you close your eyes at night. That's why each of the activities in this book is specifically designed to strengthen and hone the skills that will help you conquer each day.

Each activity has a list of skills you can boost, but you can also use the index in the back of the book to help you find activities that will help you improve a superpower you are struggling with. For example, if you struggle with focus, simply turn to the index, look up which tools and activities you can use to help with focus, pick something that sounds amazing and get to work fine-tuning your focus. Your adults won't know what got into you. I am putting the key in your hands. Now you can unlock your true potential and rock every single day!

By the end of this book you will be a rock star with the ability to fine-tune all of your inner superpowers.

Skills to help you recognize your likes and dislikes, understand all eight of your super senses and hone your **UNIQUE** set of strengths and struggles:

- Self-regulation
- Self-calming
- Self-care
- Self-awareness

Skills to challenge your **ADVENTUROUS** nature, encourage flexible thinking, push you to try new things and break down the barriers that hold you back:

- Strength
- Balance
- Flexible thinking
- Hand strength (fine motor)
- Risk taking
- Decision making
- Motor planning
- Coordination

Skills to help your grown-ups harness all of your energy, encourage positive thinking and master your **SPIRITED** moods:

- Emotional regulation
- Impulse control
- Focus
- Concentration
- Alertness
- Emotional awareness

Skills to improve your organization, boost your memory and keep you focused and on task while preserving your **CREATIVE** brain:

- Independence
- Communication
- Following directions

- Patience
- Teamwork
- Self-confidence

Skills to tame your **FIERCE** side enough to take a stand in a respectful way, become an expert on how you process information and be a champion for yourself:

- Time management
- Organization
- Self-monitoring
- Attention to detail

- Planning and prioritizing
- Working memory
- Creativity

## Train Your Adult

Look, I know what it is like to grow up in a world of big people misunderstanding you. I was just like you when I was growing up. In fact, when I was little, I used to get in trouble for talking when the teacher was talking, and even to this day, you can find me sitting behind a very messy desk that drives my mom bonkers. Now that I am an adult, I know what it's like to be on both sides of the fence. Sometimes I stare at my son and wonder, "What in the world are you doing?" Then I remember exactly what I was like when I was his age and all of the awesome science I've learned about the way his brain and body work, and suddenly I understand exactly what he is doing.

In this book, I've taken my experience as a superkid just like you and my knowledge as a grown-up and meshed them together to help you bridge the gap between being misunderstood to teaming up with the grown-ups who love you. Each activity comes with a quick guide to flip your adult's thinking and respectfully stand up for yourself and your superkid needs. I promise you, your grown-up wants to see you conquer every day just as much as you want to conquer it. Now, you have the tools to help your grown-up help you!

Are you ready to conquer your day? If so, turn the page and let's find your next adventure.

# CHAPTER 1

# ROCKIN' MORNING ROUTINES TO START YOUR DAY IN AN AWESOME MOOD

Mornings can make or break your day. Getting up on the wrong side of the bed, not having enough energy or being full of worry can make it seem like the world's biggest villains are out to get you. However, if you can learn to harness your superpowers first thing in the morning, you will skyrocket through your day! These activities will help everyone have an argument-free morning. From getting dressed to squashing those big nasty worries before you start your day, these activities will get you energized, organized and ready for an awesome day!

Have you ever noticed some of your biggest arguments with your adults happen during the morning rush? Some days it might even feel like your grown-up is around every corner, yelling for you to hurry up, do this and do that. I want to let you in on a little secret. Your grown-up hates this tension just as much as you do, and he or she would give anything to send you off each day with a hug and a kiss and a smile on everyone's face. My number one tip for helping everyone have the perfect morning is to *slow down*. While it seems counterproductive when mornings are busy and rushing, slowing down to take a deep breath or breaking your routines into small chunks will save everyone the headache of a morning fight.

# WAKING UP WITH ANIMAL WALKS

Every sleepyhead knows getting going in the morning can be the absolute pits. What if I told you that walking like an animal would get your brain and your body ready for an amazing day? Pretty cool, right? Jumping quickly like a kangaroo will give your brain and body the boost of energy it needs if you're feeling too sleepy. Crawling slowly like a crab will help you calm down if you wake up with too much energy. No matter which animal tickles your fancy, your body will thank you for pushing all the right buttons with a "just right" attitude to guide your day.

## How to Do This Activity

Find an open space in your room or somewhere fun in your house with lots of space. Pick three of your favorite animals and spend a few minutes walking, hopping and moving like those animals.

If it is a lovely day outside, you can even do these in your front yard or in the school parking lot.

## Animal Walks to Get You Started

Elephant: With your head and arms hanging down, bend forward at your waist and squeeze your hands together tightly. As you walk with your feet far apart, swing your arms back and forth like an elephant's trunk.

Kangaroo: Stand with your heels touching and your hands up to your chest. Try taking gigantic hops while keeping your heels together the whole time.

Snake: Lie on the ground and reach as far in front of you as you can. Try to slither across the room on your stomach, staying stretched out like a snake.

## How to Use This Tool

Animal walks and moves are the perfect way to calm your body or perk up your energy level. If you are looking for something to wake you up and get you moving, try being animals that jump and spin. If you need to calm down and focus, try being an animal that crawls, slithers or pushes on the ground.

(continued)

## What You Need

Your body

# WAKING UP WITH
# ANIMAL WALKS (CONT.)

## Challenge

What animals can you mimic that aren't listed? Can you move like every animal of the alphabet?

Play a game with your family or friends at school. See if they can guess the animal you are moving like.

## TRAIN YOUR ADULT ★

These activities are known as heavy work because they give your bones, muscles and joints pressure. This is very important for your proprioceptive (say: proh-pree-uh-sep-tiv) sensory system of body awareness. Since this activity can be either energizing or calming when you need it, it's great to suggest to your adult when he or she starts to get frustrated at you for jumping on the furniture, running around the house or acting grumpy, and it's the perfect antidote for after-school attitude.

# WHAT'S IN YOUR BACKPACK SHRINKY DINK® ZIPPER CHARMS

**Superpowers**
organization, attention to detail, working memory

**Sensory Systems**
sight, touch

**Energy Scale**
⚡⚡

Are you tired of forgetting everything you need in your desk? Forgetting things can make you feel downright lowly, but you will never forget your folder again after you make these awesome Shrinky Dink® zipper pulls. It's pretty amazing what happens when we give our brains a visual reminder of the things that are most important. Never again have an adult call you lazy or disorganized.

## How to Make Ahead

Start by tracing or copying the images from page 191 onto your Shrinky Dinks® paper and then coloring in your pictures with colored pencils or permanent marker. You don't need to copy each image, but make sure you get all the things you usually put in your backpack each day.

Cut out your images and use your hole puncher to put a hole at the top of your picture. Place each of your pictures on a cookie sheet and, with adult supervision, bake them in the oven for 1 to 3 minutes at 325°F (163°C). As soon as they flatten out, remove them from the oven and let them cool. You can use a spatula to flatten your charms even more if they curl on the edges.

Once your charms are cooled off, add a small connector ring before adding them to your keyring. Finally, attach your charms to the zipper pull on your backpack.

## How to Use This Tool

Never forget another thing with these zipper charms. Now when you head off to school, check everything you need off the list by thumbing through your charms. When you start to head back home, make sure you have all your belongings by doing a quick double check of your charms.

(continued)

## What You Need

Pictures of items you carry in your backpack (see page 191)

Shrinky Dinks® paper (can be purchased at most craft stores)

Colored pencils or permanent markers

Scissors

Hole puncher

Connector rings

Keyring

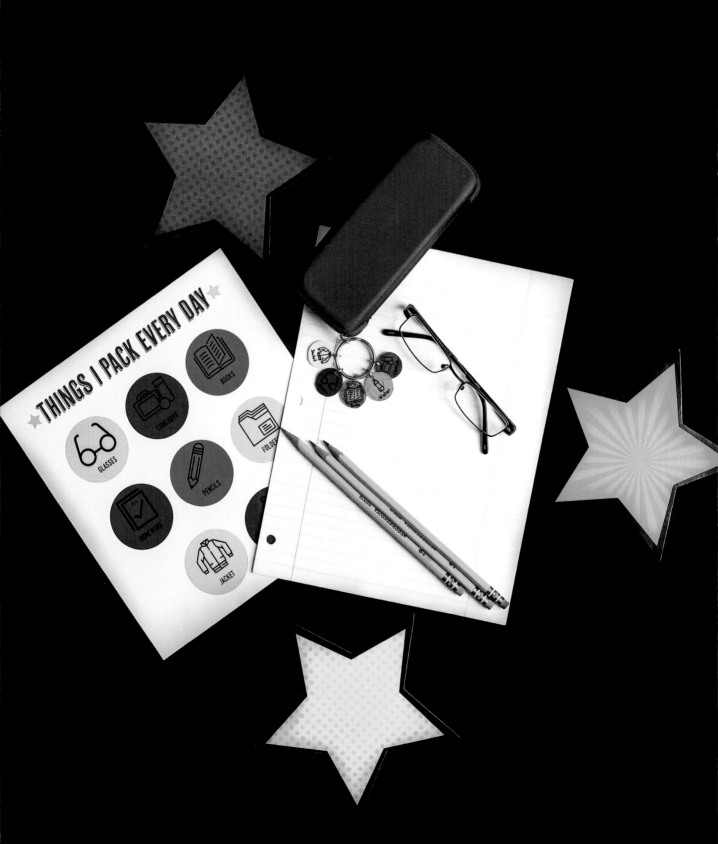

# WHAT'S IN YOUR BACKPACK
# SHRINKY DINK® ZIPPER CHARMS (CONT.)

## Challenge

Have a project where you need to remember facts? Make a set of charms to help you remember everything you need to know. Can you make a charm of the water cycle or the life cycle of frogs?

## TRAIN YOUR ADULT ★

Your brain is naturally working overtime with everything you have to remember. Remembering your folder, library books or even your lunch can completely slip your mind. Retrain adults to see that you are not being lazy. Instead, you need help with your working memory and building the brain muscles that help you stay organized. By giving you a visual to rely on, your grown-up will be able to throw the nagging away and save the chatter in the morning for reminding you how much they care about you.

# ANTI-TIME WARP TIMERS

Do you feel like you never have enough time? Or do you get in trouble for not using your time wisely? Have no fear! Not only is this handy timer super fun to make, but it is also exactly what every superhero needs to keep on track to avoid getting sucked into a time warp. Turn this bad boy over and watch the seconds move along as you knock things off your to-do list faster than a speeding bullet.

## How to Make Ahead

Start by removing the labels and lids from your plastic bottles and setting the bottles to the side for later. Use superglue to attach the lids to each other and let them dry overnight before covering the outside of the lids with duct tape.

With the help of your adult, cut 2 holes the same size as your straws in the middle of your lids and slide the straws through the holes.

Your straws should be placed so that there is one straw sticking out on each side of the lid. The opposite side of the straw should only be as long as the lid. Add silicone or waterproof glue around the straws and let them sit overnight to dry.

Now you are ready to fill one bottle with water and a few drops of food coloring all the way to the top. Put your new straw lid on top of your bottle and set to the side.

Fill your second bottle with baby oil to the top. Over a sink, gently tip the two bottles together and screw the lids on tight.

## How to Use This Tool

Have you ever seen those super mesmerizing oil timers where the drops of color slowly drip through ramps and wheels? This tool is a homemade version that all your friends will want! As you turn the bottles over, the colored liquid will magically swap places with clear oil in the bottom through the tiny straws. After you have your timer just perfect, flip it over for its first magic countdown and time how long it takes for the liquids to swap places (this will be different depending on the size of the bottles you use).

The next time your grown-ups tell you to hurry up and get moving in the morning, flip over your timer and race against the clock. Can you get dressed before the timer is up? This timer also comes in super handy when you feel frustrated or upset. Simply watch as the time passes and reset your brain so you can get ready for more awesomeness!

## TRAIN YOUR ADULT ★

Is your grown-up always hounding you to hurry up? What adults don't know is that time is a very abstract thing for a superhero like yourself. Your brain actually needs a visual reminder (a concrete example) so you can literally see the time moving along. Teaching your adult to give you a visual (say: vizh-oo-uhl) tool and a warning is a great way to make both of you happy as you transition from one activity to another.

### What You Need

2 recycled plastic bottles of the same size

Superglue

Duct tape

2 drinking straws cut to 4" (10 cm)

Cutting tool (with adult help)

Silicone gel or waterproof glue (found in the hardware store)

Water

Food coloring

Baby oil (enough to fill one plastic bottle)

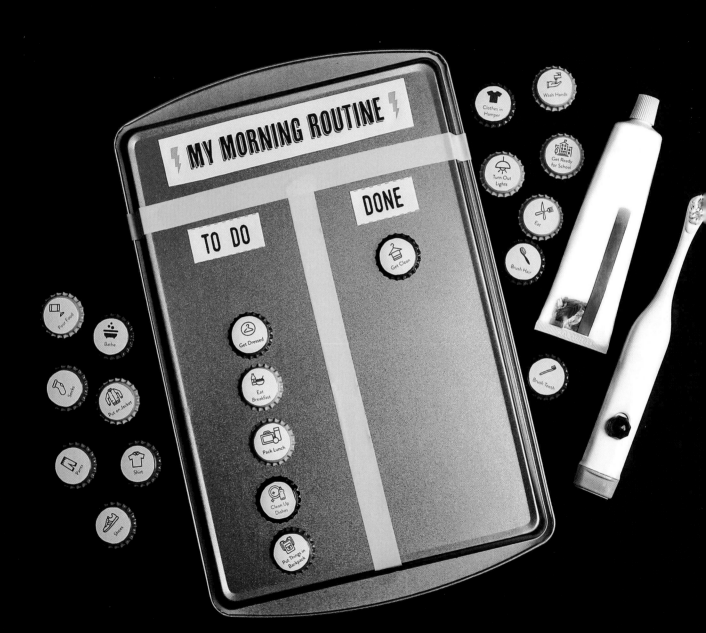

# MAGNETIC MORNING ROUTINES CHART

Every rock star knows it takes a lot to get ready for the stage. Your morning routines can be just as overwhelming. This is no fault of your own. This magnetic routine chart is great for perfecting your mornings and reducing the nagging from your adults. Have your grown-up help you brainstorm all the things you need to get done to get out the door in the morning so you can make the perfect chart. Who knows, they might want to make one for themselves when they see how well it works!

## How to Make Ahead

Cut or copy the morning routines you use each day from page 185. Using a glue stick, attach one image to the top of each of your bottle caps and set to the side to dry. With adult supervision, use hot glue to attach one magnet to the back of each bottle cap once they are dry.

With your craft tape, make a *T* shape on your cookie sheet. One side will be for routines you need "To Do" and the other side will be for "Done."

Add all of your magnets to your cookie sheet and place it next to your bed so you are ready to be awesome tomorrow morning.

## How to Use This Tool

As you complete each activity (get dressed, brush hair, brush teeth, eat breakfast, etc.), you can move your magnet to the "Done" column.

Since the chart is super portable, you can take it with you as you move through the house to keep you on track and on a roll.

## Challenge

Need a routine chart for other times of your day? Use the blank routines on page 186 to make a chart for any time of your day that needs more reminders.

## What You Need

Routine icons (page 185)

Markers

Glue stick

Clean metal bottle caps

Magnets

Hot glue (with adult supervision)

Craft tape

Cookie sheet

## TRAIN YOUR ADULT ★

Does your grown-up get frustrated in the morning when you get distracted? I bet most times you don't even realize you still have things to finish. Everyone's brain uses executive functions (say: egg-zek-yuh-tiv fuhngk-shuhnz), steps and processes that help you plan, manage and monitor your tasks. This chart is the perfect brain trainer because it breaks down your morning routine and helps you plan and manage time as you move your pieces from one side to the other! Now, you can get your morning routines done and have time for the things you want to do.

# HELLO MR. SUNSHINE MORNING STRETCHES

Sometimes Mr. Sunshine wakes up long before you do and you need a little help greeting your day with a happy attitude. These simple yoga stretches will wake up your inner super-stretchy attitude and help you be more flexible in your thinking the next time a villain appears.

## How to Use This Tool

All you need is your own body and plenty of space to get your morning started right. As soon as you hop out of bed, train your body and mind to get focused on the day with a few of the following stretches.

**Child's pose:** Kneel on the floor and bend your head over to the floor. Place your hands above your head or beside your body. Picture yourself as a stepping stone or a boulder that can't be moved by the troubles of your day.

**Downward dog:** Place your feet flat on the floor, bend forward and put your hands on the floor in front of you. You should look like an upside down V. Take some deep breaths as you look toward your belly button.

**Feet up a wall:** Just lie on your back on a bed or the floor and put your feet up against the wall to make a 90-degree angle with your body and legs.

The best part about these stretches is that they take almost no time at all to be effective. Start by spending 30 to 60 seconds on each stretch and build up stamina and strength by adding more stretches to your morning routine or by trying to hold each pose for longer periods of time. Your brain will thank you later.

## What You Need

Your body

Calm music (optional)

## TRAIN YOUR ADULT ★

Stretching and focusing is a healthy mindfulness habit. Mindfulness is the act of paying attention to your surroundings and freeing your mind so good thoughts can carry you through your day. By stretching your body, you are adding oxygen to your brain stem (which is the center for emotional control). Adding oxygen to your brain through morning stretches will not only prepare you for an amazing day, it will reduce your stress and worries in under 5 minutes a day. And, if you stretch with your grown-up, you'll be helping them have an awesome day, too!

# CALM, COOL AND COLLECTED

## Breathing Games to Start the Morning Right

Adults love to tell you to "just breathe." It's one of those phrases they are trained to use in adult academy. There's a reason, too. Breathing can be your number one defense against enemies (even your internal enemies) and can shut down any tantrum or meltdown in a flash. The problem is that even the coolest kids on the block don't naturally know how to breathe correctly. That's why these awesome breathing games are perfect for starting your day and loading your toolkit for any obstacle you might face.

### How to Use This Tool

Learning how to breath when the going gets rough is not as easy as it sounds. It takes lots of practice but I know if you try these simple breathing exercises and games, you will be on track to battle the yuck.

**Rise and Fall:** This game is played by lying on your back with your favorite stuffed animal on your stomach. Close your eyes and think of something happy (a new toy, ice cream sundaes, a day at the park, etc.). Begin to focus on your breathing. Don't take a big deep breath or breathe forcefully. Instead, simply focus on your natural breathing.

Inhale through your nose slowly and feel your belly rise. You should see your stuffed animal rise as your belly fills with air. As you are inhaling the breath, count slowly to three. Now, slowly exhale the breath and feel your belly release the oxygen and return to its original size. Do this for a few minutes, really focusing on your breath and your belly going in and out and in again.

### Challenge

Now, mix it up a bit. Using the different props (pom-poms, straws, balloons and pinwheels) try to do the same breathing game. Try to make your stuffed animal rise and fall while blowing up a balloon, spinning a pinwheel or keeping a pom-pom in the air with a straw.

### What You Need

Your body

Stuffed animal

Pom-poms

Straws

Balloons

Pinwheels

### TRAIN YOUR ADULT ★

The problem most grown-ups have when it comes to breathing is they think it's an obvious strategy that everyone knows how to use. Remember, it's been a long time since your adult was a growing superkid too. By lying on the floor and focusing on your breathing, you are teaching your grown-up the importance of getting oxygen to your brain. He or she can use your stuffed animal to gauge just how effective your breathing is. This way, your grown-up can never again assume you know how to "just breathe."

# CLEAN DETECTIVES

Some people are neat and tidy. Then there's the rest of us. No matter how much we think we clean our rooms, our adults are never happy. They can always find something we missed! Want to teach your adult something really cool and make them happy with a cleaner room? This awesome cleaning hack will get your adults off your back and give you super visual cleaning powers you never knew you had.

## How to Make Ahead

When your room is in its absolute messiest state, take pictures of each part of your room. Be sure to get a picture of your messed-up bed, the clothes on the floor, the mess under the dresser and on top of the cabinets. Save these pictures in a safe place so you can use them later.

Now, clean your room. Don't peek at the pictures just yet. Just clean like you normally do. When you think your room is all clean but you know your adult probably won't think it is clean, take a second round of pictures. Make sure you take pictures of the exact same spots as before.

Finally, have your adult help you clean to their standards. That's right, have them help you clean, just this once. With this simple hack, they will never have to help you again. Once the room is to their shiny liking, take a final set of pictures of the room.

## How to Use This Tool

All those pictures you have been taking are now the perfect images for look and find. See what is different in the clean and not-clean pictures. How many things can you spot out of place in your "clean" room before your adults helped you?

The next time you are asked to "clean your room," use your pictures as a guide to help you find all of the things that are out of place that you might have otherwise overlooked.

## Challenge

For even more fun, print out your pictures and use a black marker to circle the items that are out of place. Better yet, see if your adult can find all the items out of place. Don't be so quick to stash those photos under your bed. Instead, hang them on your wall or put them in a notebook so you can reference your clean room cheat sheets every day to keep your room cleaner before it ever turns into a disaster area. Because let's face it . . . cleaning a small mess is much easier than cleaning after a tornado!

## TRAIN YOUR ADULT ★

Grown-ups use words like *lazy* and *messy* when they talk about your cleaning because they don't know that your visual sensory system is overloaded and you can't see details in the middle of a mess. This is called visual discrimination (say: vizh-oo-uhl dih-skrim-uh-ney-shuhn). With this game, you can train your grown-up to break down the process and help you see what is still messy. Instead of sending you to your room to clean, they can say, "Clean the top of your counter, put your clothes in your drawer and make your bed." Mixing these smaller steps with photos of what "clean" means to them will help you remind them you are trying your best.

### What You Need

Camera (you can use a digital camera, cell phone or instant camera)

Printer (optional)

Black marker (optional)

# WIZARDLY WORRY STONES

Worry is a very normal thing, but it sure doesn't feel that way when your heart starts to race and your palms get sweaty. Especially in the morning when you want to be happy and excited for the new day! Cast a spell on all your worries once and for all with these simple wizardly worry stones. These small stones are perfect for rubbing away your worries. They fit discreetly in your pocket so they can easily go undetected.

## How to Make Ahead

In a large bowl, mix together the flour, salt and water until all the ingredients are evenly mixed. Next, knead the dough with your hands until the dough is moldable and pliable. Using a toothpick, add small amounts of your favorite gel color until you get the perfect color you want. Use your imagination to dream up the perfect wizardly colors.

Sprinkle in just a little bit of glitter and knead everything together one more time.

Pinch off a quarter-size ball and form it into a cube (a box with flat sides). Pinch the sides just a little so the sides dent to fit your thumb.

With adult supervision, heat your oven to 200°F (93°C) and bake for 60 minutes or until firm. You can also let them air dry for 24 to 48 hours if you don't have access to an oven.

## How to Use This Tool

Once your worry stones are dry, you can take them anywhere. They are perfect for throwing in your pocket when you have a test at school or you have to go visit relatives you haven't seen in a long time. Simply put the stones between your fingers and thumb and rub the sides for a gentle calming effect.

## Challenge

Try naming your big worries or thought monsters that are taking over your brain. Use sentences like:

"I am worried about . . . "
"I am upset because . . . "
"I am scared that . . . "

## TRAIN YOUR ADULT ★

Worries are something that all of us face one way or another. Believe it or not, even your grown-ups worry. In fact, they take it upon themselves to protect you from all your big worries and scary thoughts, but sometimes they miss the smallest thing that can be making you nervous. Instead of your adults saying, "There's nothing to worry about" (which can make you feel like they aren't truly listening to you), train them to hear your worries, acknowledge they are important and remind you to use your tools such as these Wizardly Worry Stones to whisk your worries away.

### Superpowers
communication, emotional regulation, self-calming, self-awareness

### Sensory Systems
touch, body awareness, internal cues

### Energy Scale
⚡⚡

### What You Need
1 cup (125 g) flour
1 cup (241 g) salt
½ cup (120 ml) warm water
Gel food coloring
Glitter

# FEELINGS MASKS

Have you ever woken up on the wrong side of the bed? I get it. I've been there. In fact, we all have. Having emotions and feelings is part of being who you are. Sometimes, though, you have to learn to communicate your feelings to others (like your parents) so they can see you are still your same awesome self. These masks are the perfect way to communicate your moods and emotions with your family first thing in the morning without even saying a word. Not only are they fun to make, they are the perfect tool for rockin' your mornings and connecting with adults.

## How to Make Ahead

Start by cutting out two oval shapes (eyes), two skinny rectangles (eyebrows), a triangle (nose) and a half circle (mouth) from your scrap cardboard. Using your markers, decorate these to look like your facial parts and add hair and skin color to your cardboard circle.

Now, using the brad fasteners, attach each of your facial pieces to the circle so they can move to show different emotions. Feel free to add yarn (hair), wiggly eyes and fabric to make it look more like you.

Finally, attach a Popsicle stick to the bottom of the face on the back with tape and you are ready to show your emotions.

## Challenge

Try to go beyond the basic emotions of happy, sad and mad. Try to think about what you look like when you are tired, worried, scared, overexcited or even sick. You can use the list of emotions on page 182 to help you if you get stuck.

## How to Use This Tool

Once your mask is complete and dry, put it in a safe place (like a basket on your dresser). Each day (and throughout your day), use your mask to show adults how you are feeling. This tells them how they can support you. This is a great morning habit for the whole family to do. If someone in the family is having a rough start, what can you do to help them?

## TRAIN YOUR ADULT ★

You experience a variety of emotions from day to day, and sorting through these emotions can be draining for any child. This activity is a great starting point for your adult to teach you the names of emotions, and it also reminds them to give you space and safety to feel a wide range of emotions.

**Superpowers**
confidence, emotional regulation, self-monitoring, communication

**Sensory Systems**
internal cues, sight

**Energy Scale**

**What You Need**

Circle cardboard cut-outs (or paper plates)

Markers

Brad fasteners

Yarn, wiggly eyes, fabric pieces (optional)

Popsicle sticks

Tape

# WEEKDAY ROCK STAR WARDROBE ORGANIZER

Every rock star needs an amazing wardrobe, from sparkly shirts to stellar socks. This can be a hard and frustrating task in the middle of a busy morning. From having to organize your thoughts quick enough to make a decision about your best outfit for the day to finding clothes that feel just right on your skin, getting dressed can seem like a feat that is impossible. With this weekday wardrobe organizer, you will not only save time, but you will be in charge of what you wear to school and for play while making your adults happy at the same time!

## How to Make Ahead

Start by cutting the top tabs off your cereal box. Then, glue all of the boxes together so they are stacked, lying facedown. Finally, cover the outside of the stack with your duct tape, even covering the front edges of your "shelves." Using letter stickers, add labels to each slot. Start with M for *Monday* on the top and end with F for *Friday* on the bottom.

## How to Use This Tool

This organizer is going to end all battles with your adults over clothes. On the weekend, take some time to go through your favorite clothes and pick out five shirts, five pairs of pants, socks, undies and anything else you need for your week.

Once you have your shelves filled, have your adult check to make sure he or she approves of your school-week wardrobe, so any battles happen when the stage is calm and not when you need to get ready for the show!

## Challenge

For added visual support, add pictures of what you need in each slot (shirt, pants, socks, undies, etc.) to each label.

## What You Need

5 recycled extra-large cereal boxes (all the same size)

Glue

Duct tape

Letter stickers

Your favorite clothes

## TRAIN YOUR ADULT ★

Train your adult to help reduce the amount of choices you have to make during the morning rush and everyone will be in a rock-star mood to start the day. By making the decisions together on the weekend when there is a lot more time for disagreements, both you and your grown-up are more likely to be happy with your rock-star wardrobe options on a busy morning. Talk to your grown-up about the scratchy tag, the prickly seam in the sock or the too-loose pants now, so you can enjoy a hassle-free morning later this week.

# WONDER WIPEROOS

Superpowers
self-care,
independence

Sensory Systems
touch

Energy Scale
⚡⚡⚡⚡

When I asked adults the single most troublesome skill they struggle to teach their little wizards, the answer was unanimous: wiping. I know, I know . . . gross. You see, it's a pretty important skill but none of us really wants to talk about it. Until now. Let's get down and dirty and use our tactile (say: tak-til) sense of touch to get to the bottom of things and win the war on wiping!

## How to Make Ahead

Blow up one large balloon about halfway (leave room for you to change the size of the balloon). If you are the type of kid that likes to get messy, use your finger to put a dab of peanut butter on the front of the balloon. If you don't like the way things feel on your fingers, use a spoon to do this step.

## How to Use This Tool

Now it's time to gross out your adult. Have them hold the top and bottom of the balloon and pull in opposite directions. It should squeeze the balloon together and form a crease in the front where the peanut butter is.

Your job is to use the toilet paper squares to practice wiping the crease of the balloon. Can you get it all on one wipe?

This activity is the perfect way to test the perfect amount of pressure you should apply when getting clean. Too much pressure and you could pop the balloon, not enough and you won't get clean. While this activity is a little on the gross side, it can really be a great way to practice something every single one of us does every day. Staying clean is important but not always easy.

## What You Need

1 large balloon

1 tbsp (11 g) peanut butter

Toilet paper squares

## Challenge

Turn this into a fun science project. Which brand of toilet paper takes the least number of wipes? Does the shape of the balloon make a difference? Who in your family can get the balloon the cleanest?

## TRAIN YOUR ADULT ★

Talking about these things is never fun for anyone. I can assure you, just as much as you don't want to talk to your adult about it, your grown-up is cringing at the thought of talking to you about your dirty undies. Make the conversation fun with this simple activity that will get you both smiling! Who knows? It might just open the door to chat about other difficult topics and help your grown-up understand your struggles a little bit better.

# FLICK 'N' FLOSS

I'm sure you've heard your adults harp on just how important it is to floss. There's a reason! Every time you eat, bacteria (say: bak-TEER-ee-uh) goes crazy munching on the sugar on your teeth and becomes a thin film known as plaque (say: plak). Eww. Right? The good news is one of the easiest ways to cut down this nasty film is to floss daily. Flossing has never been so fun and easy as it is with this awesome activity! After you play this game, you will be a flossing wiz and ready to flick that plaque away.

## How to Make Ahead

For this activity, you are going to pretend the building-block pegs are your teeth. Using your playdough, fill the space between the pegs on your block with "plaque." Then, grab the yarn with both hands and use your yarn as floss. Pull the yarn between the pegs back and forth to get all the playdough out.

## How to Use This Tool

This is not an activity to pull out during your busy bathroom routines; however, it will make you a stellar flosser so you can protect your pearly whites. Not only will this strengthen your hands, but it will help you see on a large scale what happens when you floss, to reduce any fears you have of putting the string in your mouth.

## What You Need

Large building blocks with pegs

Playdough (for homemade see page 106)

Yarn

## Challenge

Set a timer and see if you can beat your time but still get all the playdough out from the "teeth."

Set up a super challenge by doing this with a blindfold on. Can you still get your teeth just as clean?

If you are looking for rock-star moves to try during your flossing, try involving your supersonic auditory (say: aw-di-tawr-ee) sense of hearing to hum a tune to pass the time and take your mind off the feeling of the string in your mouth.

## TRAIN YOUR ADULT ★

If you hate flossing, use this activity as a stepping-stone to sharing with your adult what you don't like. Is it that you don't understand how to do it? Is it that you hate the feel of the string in your mouth? Are you worried something is going to happen when you floss? The easiest way to calm any frustrations between you and your adult when he or she asks you to floss is to be open and tell him or her what you need.

If the feel of string in your mouth sends chills down your spine, let your grown-up know so he or she can gradually (slowly) introduce you to the feel of the string. This activity is perfect for getting the string in your hands and helping you see what is happening in your mouth when you floss.

# CHAPTER 2

# MAGICAL MEALTIME SOLUTIONS EVEN PICKY EATERS WILL LOVE

Mealtime can be such a struggle. For some kids it might even be as bad as kryptonite is to Superman. Adults want you to be strong and healthy, but sometimes they just don't know how to help you battle those mealtime villains. They need your help!

These activities and recipes will help you love everything about mealtime. From table manners to tasty, healthy snacks for picky eaters, these activities will get you to try new foods, enjoy mealtime with your family and be ready for an awesome meal.

Mealtime can be a struggle for both superkids and grown-ups alike. You might not realize it, but your adult dreads meals each day because he or she isn't sure if today is the day you will hate toast or the day you will refuse to eat your veggies.

My number one rock-star tip for ending battles over food is to focus on flexibility and exploration. I encourage you to explore a variety of foods with all of your senses and muster all of your flexible thinking skills, put on a brave face and be willing to try new foods (even if they are green and mushy). Remember, Rome wasn't built in a day, and your taste buds won't be either. Remind your grown-ups to be patient with you as you develop your own unique mealtime preferences.

SUPERKID TIP

# COLORFUL MEALTIME MEDLEY

Have you ever heard adults talk about "picky eaters"? It's a term used for superkids like you who are very particular about what you will and will not eat. It worries adults because they know you need food to be awesome. If you struggle to try new foods, you are not alone. I've got just the game for you. Sometimes the key to trying new foods is to make the food visually exciting. Grouping your foods by color can expand your go-to foods. Who knows? You might even find a new favorite!

## How to Make Ahead

To make your spinner, divide a plate into 6 equal parts (like a pizza) and draw lines with a black marker. Color each section one color of the rainbow (red, orange, yellow, green, blue, purple).

To make your dinner plates, create a plate for each person who is playing by dividing the paper plate into 6 equal parts and drawing lines with a black marker. Do not color your plate.

Set out a tray with each of the colors of foods. Pick 2 to 3 choices from each color to add to your tray so there are several options when you play. Choose some very familiar foods and a few that are brand-new to you. These foods can be cooked or raw to fully explore many different options. Here are some ideas for each color:

RED: red peppers, strawberries, raspberries, tomatoes, watermelon, pomegranates

ORANGE: oranges, carrots, apricots, pumpkin, squash, sweet potatoes

YELLOW: bananas, squash, golden apples, yellow peppers, star fruit, pineapples, corn

GREEN: kiwis, spinach, pears, kale, cucumbers, green beans, edamame, zucchini, celery

BLUE: blueberries, currants, grapes, prunes, blackberries

PURPLE: cabbage, raisins, purple cauliflower, plums, eggplant, beets

## What You Need

Paper plates

Markers

Circular serving tray

A variety of foods from each color of the rainbow

Pencil

Paper clip

(continued)

# COLORFUL MEALTIME MEDLEY (CONT.)

## How to Use This Tool

After you have set up your colorful meal on the table, it is time to play. Each player takes a turn spinning by placing a pencil through the paper clip in the middle of the plate. Spin the paper clip to see what color it lands on. The player chooses one piece of food from that color to add to their plate. Continue having each player spin until everyone has something in every color on their plate.

Now, everyone has to try at least one bite from each of the foods they picked.

## Challenge

Each time you play this, try expanding the foods you are willing to try. Whether it is in the foods you choose to put out in the first place or the foods you choose to put on your plate, expand your choices by at least one food each time you play.

Play a round where everything you eat is from one color group.

Play a round blindfolded and guess which color you are eating.

## TRAIN YOUR ADULT ★

Having particular tastes when it comes to food can be frustrating for both you and your adult. Encourage your grown-up to introduce new foods in fun ways like this game and to be patient as you expand the collection of foods you are willing to try. The only way to unstick a sticky brain is to train it with gradual exposure and breaking normal routines (your normal evening foods). Remind your adult this won't happen overnight, but it will happen! And hey, who knows? You might actually find some new favorites when you open up your mind to try a new food.

# DYNAMITE DINNER TABLE CONVERSATION JAR

**Superpowers**
reading, turn taking, patience, self-awareness, communication

**Sensory Systems**
sight, hearing, touch

**Energy Scale**
⚡⚡⚡⚡

Sometimes sitting at the dinner table can feel like sitting behind an interrogation table. Your grown-ups constantly asking, "How was your day?" only to be met with the ever-popular response, "Fine." This Dynamite Dinner Table Conversation Jar game will blast your conversation skills to the next world, making you the talk of the table. Not only will you get to tell everyone the coolest tricks you did for the day, but you'll start connecting with your family in a whole new way!

## What You Need

Recycled glass jar

Permanent markers

Popsicle sticks

## How to Make Ahead

Color a creative pattern on the outside of a clean glass jar using permanent markers. You can be as creative as you want: make a rainbow, make stripes, make a funny face, add a super-powered symbol . . . really, the sky is the limit.

Once you have covered your entire jar, set it to dry while you prepare your conversation starters.

On each of your Popsicle sticks, write simple word clues or questions to help you the next time you are stuck and don't know what to talk about (ideas listed on the next page).

When you have enough choices, add your Popsicle sticks to your jar and place it in the middle of your dinner table.

## How to Use This Tool

At your next family meal, when your adults ask, "What did you do today?" instead of saying, "Nothing," you can pull a prompt from the jar and get the conversation rolling. Never again feel like you are at a loss for words or worried about what to talk about when you have company over.

(continued)

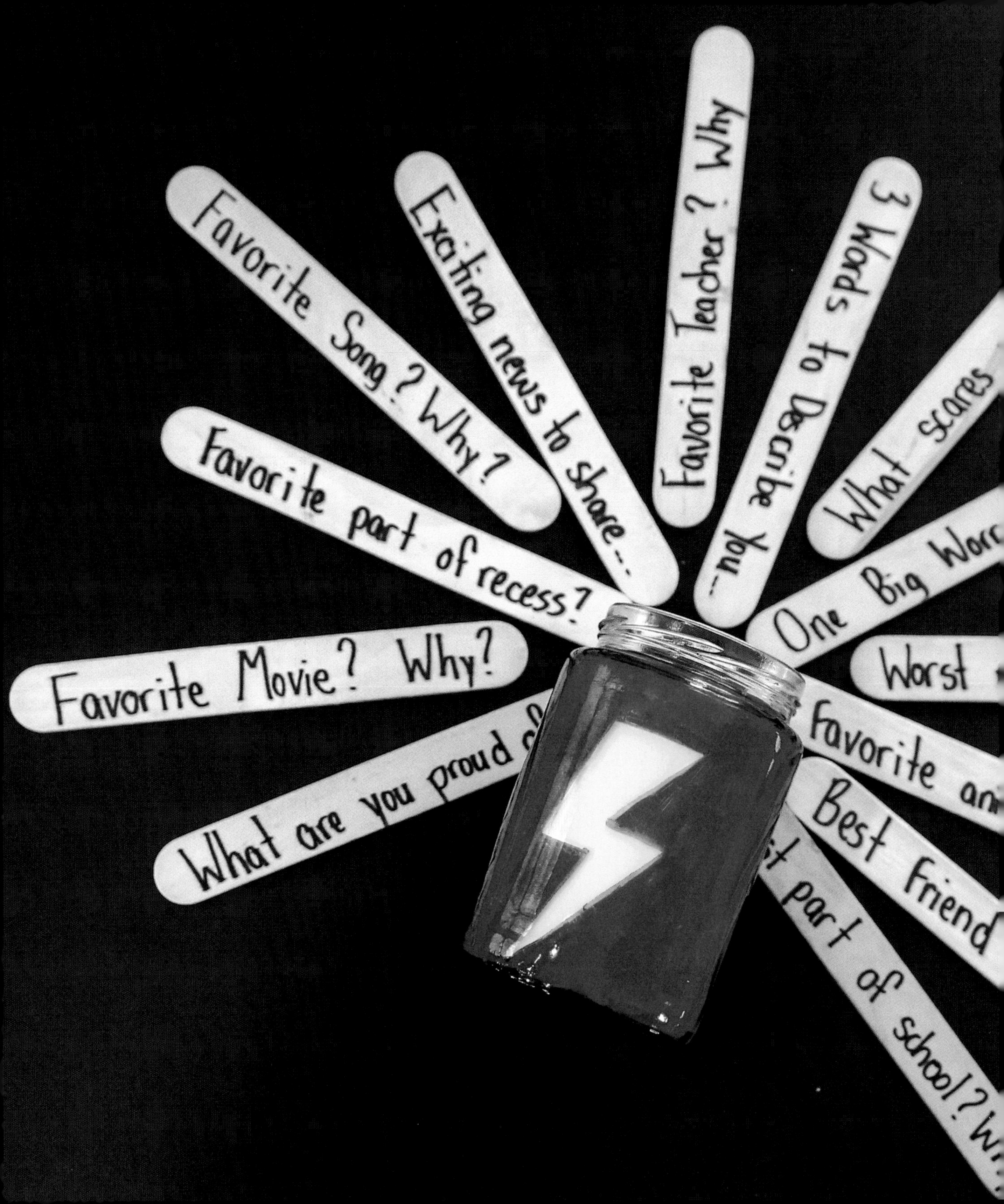
Favorite Song? Why?
Exciting news to share...
Favorite Teacher? Why
3 Words to Describe you...
What scares
One Big
Worst
Favorite part of recess?
Favorite Movie? Why?
What are you proud
Favorite
Best Friend
part of school?

# DYNAMITE DINNER TABLE CONVERSATION JAR (CONT.)

Let's learn about your day. Today, what is your favorite...

*subject in school? game you played at recess? book you read? thing you did with a friend? part of the day? WHY?*

Let's learn more about everyone. What is your favorite...

*food? movie? song? color? game? WHY?*

Let's learn about your dreams. What would you do if...

*you had a million dollars? you had to move to a new state? your friend switched schools? you lost your two front teeth? WHY?*

Let's learn about your struggles. Today, what is your...

*biggest worry? worst memory? scariest moment? WHY?*

## Challenge
Make your own conversation starters. Use cardstock paper and pens to write out some funny questions or jokes to get the conversation going with your family.

Have you ever felt like the cat's got your tongue? Adults use that phrase when kids suddenly go quiet. Your grown-up wants nothing more than to understand you, and some days that seems impossible when all of their questions are met with roadblocks. I know you have a lot to say, but you just aren't sure how to access all the awesome things you want to tell your adults. Instead of leaving adults baffled at your silence, give them this super-secret tool to get you talking and sharing all the cool things you have to say, and give them a sneak peek into your world.

# BRAIN-BOOSTING SNACK PACKS

Have you ever noticed just how awesome you feel after a healthy lunch or snack? You feel ready to take on the world and battle your biggest villains! Yet, other times you feel like you are dragging, your thoughts start to wander and your energy is zapped. This Brain-Boosting Snack Pack will feed your brain muscle with crunchy and chewy snack choices so you can always feel the boost of energy no matter where you are or what obstacles you face.

## How to Make Ahead
Clean and sanitize your craft case before getting started. Then, pick some of your favorite snacks from the list to the right and fill each section of your container with a different snack. Make sure to put in a good mix of crunchy and chewy, sweet and sour, salty and plain snacks.

## How to Use This Tool
Take this snack pack on a car trip, a trip to the park or your next outing or keep it at home for when you need a pick-me-up and a little more focus.

## Challenge
Try to add at least one snack you have never tried before each time you fill your pack.

## TRAIN YOUR ADULT ★

It might come as a surprise, but adults reach for snacks all the time when they are working. Remind your adult that healthy snacks aren't just yummy treats, but the right snack can actually wake up your brain. Crunchy foods wake us up because we have to work harder to chew and digest them (using our proprioceptive [say: proh-pree-uh-sep-tiv] sense of body awareness). Putting your jaw through a workout is just what your brain needs to stay alert the next time you need a boost of focus and attention. The truth is, the more senses we use when we eat, the more alert we can become.

## What You Need
Small craft case with compartments

Crunchy snacks: pretzels, almonds, cashews, dried edamame, sunflower seeds, popcorn

Chewy snacks: dried apricots, dried cranberries, raisins

# SQUEEZE-AND-SIP WATERMELON SLUSHIES

Are you an awesome kiddo that seeks out as much sensory input as you can find? It's okay. Some of us are hardwired in our brains to touch, feel, smell and even taste everything we are around. It's how you get the most out of your world. These squeeze-and-sip slushies are perfect for your incredibly active sensory appetite.

## How to Make Ahead

Start by decorating your bag by drawing several "watermelon seeds" with a black marker. After your adult has sliced up your watermelon into small chunks, fill your bags with watermelon, leaving a little room for movement. Close your bag and start to squeeze and squash your watermelon. Once your watermelon is nice and mushy, add the lemonade and reseal your bag. Place in the freezer for 1 hour (or until your drink becomes slushy). Place a straw in your bag, and you are ready to enjoy!

## How to Use This Tool

These squeeze-and-sip slushies are perfect for a warm day or an afternoon at the park. If you are a kid who loves to push, pull and squeeze, this is the perfect snack for you to make. Get in your proprioceptive (say: proh-pree-uh-sep-tiv) input by mushing up the watermelon to a pulp. Don't like to get messy? This is a perfect introduction to messy food because you have the bag to protect you while you play with your food.

Finally, this is a great snack for kids who love to bite, chew and suck on their fingers. It gives you something tasty and delicious to put in your mouth and sends healthy signals to your brain at the same time!

## What You Need

Small plastic bag

Permanent marker

½ cup (76 g) watermelon chunks

½ cup (120 ml) lemonade

Straw

## TRAIN YOUR ADULT ★

Want to know a supersonic secret that will blow your grown-up's mind? Not only is this snack great for playing with your food, but it is incredibly helpful to boost focus and attention. When you have to suck foods through a straw, you force your brain to pay close attention to the world around you and increase your alertness. So the next time your grown-up goes to grab you a snack, encourage him or her to get one you can suck through a straw (such as fruit pouches, water bottles and milk). It can be our secret that drinking milkshakes through a straw can boost your brain!

# RACE TO THE FINISH DINNERTIME GAMEBOARD

Mealtime can be such a drag. You know what you like and don't like, you are even willing to try new foods, but mealtime just seems to go on forever. What if we made a game of it, and at the end of your meal you got your favorite treat of all? Fun, right? It will make trying new foods worth it! Train your adults with this super fun dinnertime game that is sure to put you in the "clean plate club."

## How to Make Ahead

Tear out or copy the gameboard from page 189. If you want it to last longer, you can laminate the board or cover it with clear packing tape. Set the game board next to you at dinnertime and place your bottle cap on the start position. If other people in your family want to play along, have them copy the game board and play along with their plate, too. The whole family can play side by side for this one!

## How to Use This Tool

As you eat your dinner, follow the instructions on the game board and move your game piece along the path. You get to move ahead for each bite of familiar food you take until you reach a challenge square (*Bam!*). These squares are meant to encourage you to try one thing from your plate that is unfamiliar or undesirable (not your favorite). Keep going on the path until you reach the treat at the end!

## Challenge

Each time you play, add more foods that you normally don't eat.

## TRAIN YOUR ADULT ★

Have you ever heard your adult tell you to "quit being so picky" or "take another bite," and you wished they knew how hard it is for you to try new foods? End these power struggles by working together to create a meal everyone is happy with. You will need to be a little flexible and willing to eat foods you don't love, and your grown-up will need to believe that you won't starve and will eat when you are ready. If your adult calls you a picky eater, this is the perfect game to surprise them with your willingness to try new things. Plus, there's a treat for you at the end!

## What You Need

Race to the Finish Gameboard (page 189)

A bottle cap (or something else as a game piece)

Your dinner

A small treat your adult agrees on (this can be something simple like your favorite fruit or a small cookie)

# SMELLIVISION

## Guess That Food

**Superpowers**
attention to detail, concentration, risk taking, self-awareness

**Sensory Systems**
smell

**Energy Scale**
↯ ↯ ↯ ↯

Have you ever noticed that foods on TV look so delicious but when you actually have those foods in front of you on the dinner table your nose immediately turns to the ceiling? Not only is this frustrating to your grown-up, leaving them feeling like they can never please you, but it can also leave you moody and angry because the only words you can muster are "I don't like it" when really you want to say so much more. This game is the perfect way to hone your super sniffer and become a detective. The next time you are faced with a food you don't like, you will know exactly why and be armed with the knowledge to expand your thinking and try new foods that otherwise might go bad on your plate.

## How to Make Ahead

To make your old-fashioned television, start by cutting out a rectangle frame from your cardboard as the frame of the television and then paint knobs and buttons along the side. Next, twist together the aluminum foil to make two long antennae and attach to the top of the cardboard using your tape. If you want your television to look more realistic, you can cover the opening in the middle with black felt and cut a slit big enough for your hand to fit through in the center.

## How to Use This Tool

This game is best played with more than one player. One player puts on the blindfold while the other player holds one of the foods in the television. The player with the blindfold then guesses the food using only the sense of smell.

## Challenge

Try foods not listed for an extra challenge. Can you think of some super smelly foods that might trick your friends?

## TRAIN YOUR ADULT ★

Did you know that your olfactory (say: ol-fak-tuh-ree) sense of smell influences many decisions throughout your life? When we learn to hone in on which smells we like or don't like and how they make us feel, we have words that can help us stand up for ourselves and help our adults understand us a little better (not just with meals). Use this activity to explore the smells of foods you like and dislike. Who knows? Your adult might learn something about his or her preferences as well.

## What You Need

Cardboard

Paint

Aluminum foil

Tape

Black felt (optional)

Blindfold

Smelly foods: onion, orange, cinnamon, chocolate chip cookies, lemon, fresh bread, freshly popped popcorn, vanilla extract, pepper shaker

# TERRIFIC TASTE BUD TESTERS

Supertasters to the rescue! Did you know that when you eat food, you use more than just your sense of taste? It's true. This activity will test your senses to the max. Not only will you identify the way things taste, but you will pay attention to how things smell and feel while noticing if your food is pushing back against you. Knowing what you like and don't like will boost your powers and give you strength to stand for your likes and dislikes using cool words like *proprioceptive* (say: proh-pree-uh-sep-tiv) and *gustatory* (say: guhs-tuh-tawr-ee). Helping adults understand everything your brain is doing when you eat your next meal will help them plan the perfect meals and see why sometimes meals just aren't something you enjoy.

## How to Use This Tool

Gather at least ten foods to compare and play with at a time. As you take a test bite, think about all of your senses. The goal is to name as many things about this one food as you can.

How does it **taste**? Sweet, salty, sour, spicy, tangy, bitter, etc.

How does it **feel**? Crunchy, mushy, slimy, watery, cold, hot, juicy, etc.

How does it **smell**? Fresh, old, plain, earthy, sweet, buttery, spicy, etc.

How does it **look**? Green, red, big, small, flat, round, fluffy, hard, etc.

Finally, decide if you like or don't like the food you are testing. Work to be specific about your likes and dislikes, focusing on features, textures or senses that stand out to you. The more specific you can be, the better your grown-up can plan meals you'll actually eat. Soon, mealtime might actually be something you both look forward to!

## Challenge

Play a game where your friend or adult has to close his or her eyes and guess what you are describing based on your answers to the questions above.

## TRAIN YOUR ADULT ★

When you bite your next cookie, think about all the senses you're using. You smell the chocolate with your olfactory (say: ol-fak-tuh-ree) sense, you taste the sweetness with your gustatory (say: guhs-tuh-tawr-ee) sense, you feel the crumbles against your tongue and cheeks with your tactile (say: tak-til) sense and you receive signals to your brain when you crunch using your proprioceptive (say: proh-pree-uh-sep-tiv) sense. This is a lot of information to take in at one time. If you really want to help your adult hone in on one sense at a time, try the Colorful Mealtime Medley game on page 45 to fine-tune your visual (say: vizh-oo-uhl) sense of sight or the Smellivision activity on page 57 to dial in on your olfactory (say: ol-fak-tuh-ree) sense of smell.

**Superpowers**
attention to detail, risk taking, self-awareness, communication

**Sensory Systems**
taste, touch, smell, hearing, body awareness

**Energy Scale**
⚡⚡⚡⚡

## What You Need

Foods from your pantry and refrigerator

# MEGA MEALTIME DECISION BOARDS

Making decisions for meals can leave even the most decisive wizard speechless. Too many choices and not enough time can be the combination for a mealtime meltdown. The internal battle of whether you should choose apples or oranges as your fruit seems so small but can overwhelm your brain and shut your decision-making ability down. Neither you nor your adults wants that to happen. Rock your mealtime decisions with this choice board that will jumpstart your decision making with a visual booster.

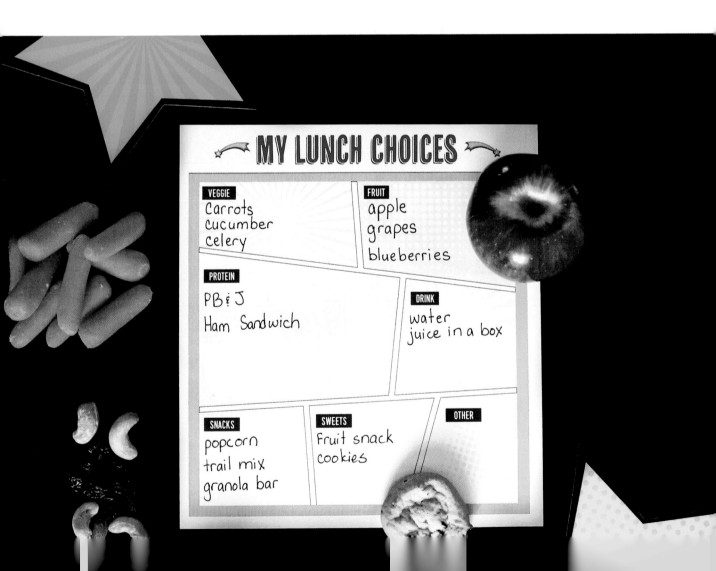

## ★ MY LUNCH CHOICES ★

**VEGGIE**
Carrots
cucumber
celery

**FRUIT**
apple
grapes
blueberries

**PROTEIN**
PB&J
Ham Sandwich

**DRINK**
water
juice in a box

**SNACKS**
popcorn
trail mix
granola bar

**SWEETS**
Fruit snack
cookies

**OTHER**

## How to Make Ahead

Copy or tear out the mealtime decision board on page 187. You can use it directly out of the book or "laminate" it by covering it with a layer of clear packing tape on the front and back so you can use it over and over again.

Once you have your decision board ready, choose a meal in which decision making is hardest for you. A lot of awesome kids struggle to pick their lunch.

With your adult, brainstorm at least three options for each food group and write them on your decision board. You will need to be flexible and work with your grown-up to create a list based on foods you already have in your house or items they are willing to add to the grocery list for the week. If you are a kid who works best with pictures, you can draw pictures on your chart.

Use a magnet to hang this on your refrigerator or keep it on the counter close to your pantry for your next mealtime decisions.

## How to Use This Tool

The next time you are at a loss for what to eat and can't make up your mind, take a peek at your decision board for a visual reminder of what is behind those closed doors. Pick one item from each of your food groups for a healthy and well-rounded meal.

This is perfect for packing lunch boxes or making your own breakfast.

## Challenge

Go ahead and make a few copies of this decision board so you can have one for breakfast, lunch, dinner and snacks.

### TRAIN YOUR ADULT ★

The truth is, when you linger in front of the fridge or cabinets, your grown-ups start to get antsy. By engaging your visual (say: vizh-oo-uhl) sense of sight, your brain will be able to quickly scan the meal-choice board and make an informed decision. Not only will this make your decision making smoother, it will cut down the arguments about what to eat with your grown-up, so you can have more time to connect and enjoy your adult.

**Superpowers**
independence, planning and prioritizing, working memory, decision making

**Sensory Systems**
sight

**Energy Scale**
⚡⚡

## What You Need

Mealtime Decision Board (page 187)

Clear packing tape (optional)

Dry-erase markers

# MARVELOUSLY MOODY PIZZAS

This will be the happiest and saddest meal you will have at the same time. This is one way to eat your way through your moods. Much like the Feelings Masks on page 34, these pizzas are the perfect way to learn about emotions while having fun at the same time. Plus, this is a meal win for both you and your grown-up. This dinner-with-a-purpose will be a meal you will beg your grown-ups to make, and they can feel good making it often because of the good-for-you ingredients and the moody payoff!

## How to Make Ahead

In a small bowl, dissolve the sugar and yeast in the water and let it sit for about 10 minutes. Stir in the salt, oil and flour. Knead the dough on a floured surface with your hands until it isn't sticky anymore. Grease a large bowl with olive oil and place your dough in it. Cover it with a towel and let it double in size (about an hour).

Next, punch your dough down and roll it out. Let it sit another 10 minutes. Roll it one more time, this time on a pizza pan. Bake for about 10 minutes at 400°F (204°C). Add your spaghetti sauce and cheese to your precooked base and you are ready to make your Marvelously Moody Pizzas.

Use your toppings to make a face that shows one of the moods or feelings from page 182.

Bake for 4 to 6 more minutes at 400°F (204°C) until the crust is a nice golden brown.

## How to Use This Tool

These make the perfect dinner or playdate meal. Have a blast trying to make as many emotions and moods as you can think of. Think about what your eyebrows do when you are angry. What does your mouth look like when you are excited? Can you make your pizza face look like you feel? Use the list of emotions on page 182 for more ideas.

## Challenge

Cut the pizza dough into four parts when it is done rising and make mini pizzas with different moods. See if your adults can guess the moods you are making.

## What You Need

1 tbsp (15 g) sugar

1½ tbsp (10 g) granulated yeast

2¾ cups (660 ml) lukewarm water

1½ tbsp (24 g) coarse salt

¼ cup (60 ml) olive oil

6½ cups (815 g) all-purpose flour

Spaghetti sauce

Mozzarella cheese

Pizza toppings such as olives, red peppers, pepperoni, mushrooms, sausage

## TRAIN YOUR ADULT ★

Did you know over 40 percent of kids don't ever learn the skill of regulating their emotions? However, with a little bit of practice, as you grow stronger and older, your emotional awareness (the ability to recognize your emotions) will also get stronger and stronger. This is a delicious way to put your feelings into words so others can understand you a little better, while adding a winning recipe to the dinner rotation.

# CHAPTER 3

# WHIZZ-BANG WAITING HACKS FOR SMOOTH AND EASY TRANSITIONS

Waiting is for the birds. What superhero has time to wait around at the doctor's office or at a restaurant for a meal to arrive? Don't adults know there is awesomeness to be done and waiting just sucks all the fun out of your day? I've got just the hacks for all that waiting! These activities and crafts will help you wait patiently, avoid boredom and manage changes in your day. From travel kits to boredom busters, these activities will keep you alert, engage your senses and enable you to stay awesome all day long.

Do your eyes automatically begin to roll into the back of your head at the thought of having to wait? What if I told you that your grown-up feels exactly the same way you do? They know that you hate waiting and your body gets antsy and your moods get groggy when you have to wait too long. The problem is they don't have the antidote to combat the waiting struggles . . . until now. The number one secret strategy for getting through any wait time is engagement. Engage your brain in thinking games, engage your fingers in activity, engage your body in movement (even if it's super small movements) and engage your moods in calming strategies to pass the time along.

# RADICAL RESTAURANT GAMES

Have you ever been to a restaurant with your adults only to have to wait and wait some more? Some restaurants seem to take forever to get your food to you, right? Don't fret! These radical engineering games will boost your patience (say: pey-shuhns), otherwise known as your ability to wait calmly. No need to pack anything special. Just use the items at your table for loads of fun while you wait.

## How to Use This Tool

Waiting for your food to arrive is no fun, but there are tons of games that you can do with the items you have on your dinner table. Here are four simple games to get you started.

**#1 Tic-Tac-Toe:** You can make this classic game using four coffee stirrers as your game board and two different-colored sugar packets as your X and O pieces. Simply lay two coffee stirrers next to each other with a space in between and lay two more across them sideways to make a tic-tac-toe board. Take turns trying to get three in a row with your sugar packets.

**#2 Creamer Engineering:** Using coffee creamers, see who at the table can build the tallest tower.

**#3 Magic Man:** Surprise your whole family with this one. Take a quick trip to the restroom to put a drop of soap on your finger. Once back at the table, pour a little bit of water into a flat plate and sprinkle black pepper in the center. Touch the center of your pepper with your soapy finger and watch the magic happen. If you need this plate for your meal, don't forget to use your napkin to give it a good cleaning before you start eating. Most restaurants will be happy to bring you a new plate.

**#4 Growing Snakes:** When you open your straw, push the paper together to one end. It should be scrunched up really small. Place the straw paper on a plate. Next, dip your straw into your water glass all the way and place your finger on the top. Keeping your finger on your straw, position it above the straw paper and release the water. Watch the paper become a wiggling snake.

## Challenge

What other classic games can you make with the items you have at your dinner table? Can you play a game of I Spy or 20 Questions? What about a quick game of jelly stacking? Have you ever tried to fold your napkin into different animals?

## What You Need

Game #1: Coffee stirrers, sugar packets

Game #2: Creamers

Game #3: Plate, water, pepper, hand soap

Game #4: Straws, water, plate

## TRAIN YOUR ADULT ★

When you are bored and in need of movement at a restaurant, all your grown-up sees is a wiggly, antsy kid. Something about the way adults' brains are wired causes this to make their skin crawl. They might tell you to sit still or to just be patient. Now you can encourage them to help you keep your fingers and mind busy with fun games that will bring you together.

# OUT OF THIS WORLD FIDGET BRACELET

Fashion with a purpose—now that's what I am talking about. Here's something you will want to take note of and save for your adults when they tell you to quit fiddling with your pencil, or they want you to sit still and focus. These beaded fidget bracelets are the perfect accessory for superheroes during their day jobs. When you aren't fighting crime, you have to do boring things like schoolwork and paying attention in class. Now you can wear this supersonic bracelet, focus on your daily work and still have a little out-of-this-world distraction to keep your mind sharp.

## How to Make Ahead

Measure your black elastic to 18 inches (45 cm) and then triple the string back over this section (do not cut them apart yet). Hold all of your strings together at the top and make a knot (this should leave you with one lonely string and a loop on top of your knot). This will be your clasp when you are done. Now, cut the strings apart at the bottom so you have three separate long pieces.

String one bead on each of the strings and push to the top. Holding all the strings together just under the beads, make a new knot.

Repeat this 4 to 5 times until you get to the desired length of the bracelet.

To finish off the bracelet, add one bead to one of the strings and then tie all the strings together in a knot under that bead. Cut off any extra string. Use this bead to fasten your bracelet by pushing the bead through the clasp you made earlier.

## How to Use This Tool

This fidget bracelet can be worn to give you extra sensory input or for fashion. When you start to drift away during reading, run your fingers through the beads, pull on the elastic, or move the beads to new positions. Make it a goal to continue to focus on what you are currently doing, so the fidget is an aid and not a distraction.

## Challenge

Try making your bracelet with beads of different types and sizes. You will see that you have a preference for the feel of different textures in your fingers and against your skin.

If you don't like the feel of the bracelet but love the idea of a fidget you can take to school, add a keyring to the end and attach this to your belt loop for a simple under-desk fidget.

## What You Need

Black elastic string

Small beads (we used blue and purple "galaxy" beads)

## TRAIN YOUR ADULT ★

One of the easiest ways to calm busy fingers when waiting gets hard is to make a fidget (say: fij-it), or small tool used to provide sensory input and strengthen hand muscles. There are many many types (check out the Rainbow Nuts and Bolts Fidget on page 73). Scientists have found that doing small distracting tasks is actually good for focus and attention. When your grown-up begs you to quit fidgeting, they want you to pay attention and stay focused. By keeping tools like this fidget bracelet handy, you can fidget and focus at the same time. And you've got science on your side!

# MOVEMENT MEMORY

Every superkid needs to move. In fact, you need to move everything from your toes to your head. But what happens when you are somewhere where you have to wait for a long time and movement is limited? What you need is a simple game that can keep your body and brain active without causing too much commotion. This is a super easy game to play while you are waiting in a long line or before an event starts. Your grown-up will love the fact that you are staying busy instead of whining and asking, "How much longer?"

## How to Use This Tool

This game can be played with as few as two players and as many as an entire class of superkids.

The game starts with the first person making a movement and the next person repeating that movement. Then the second player adds a new movement to the sequence. The following player has to repeat both movements and add his or her own. The game continues until a player misses one of the movements in the sequence.

Here is an example of how a game might look:

Player One: Tap toe.

Player Two: Tap toe. Touch head.

Player Three: Tap toe. Touch head. Spin around

Player One: Tap toe. Touch head. Spin around. Jump on one foot.

Build your working memory (the function of the brain that helps you remember facts) while boosting your superpowers with a quick and simple game of Movement Memory. Will you be able to remember what movement you did last?

## Challenge

Add music to the game and challenge the players to move to the beat of the music.

## TRAIN YOUR ADULT ★

Training your adult to play movement games with you while you wait will pass the time, and it will also strengthen your muscles and make you stronger for your next big mission. Did you know that moving will actually build your brain muscles and make you even more of a rock star when it comes time to show your endurance (say: en-doo-r-uh-ns) or your ability to work for long periods of time?

**Superpowers**
following directions, working memory, motor planning, strength, planning and prioritizing, balance, endurance

**Sensory Systems**
movement, body awareness

**Energy Scale**
♪♪♪♪♪♪♪

## What You Need
Your body

At least 1 friend

Music (optional)

# RAINBOW NUTS AND BOLTS FIDGET

As much as I know you love listening to your grown-up go on and on, I also know that sometimes his or her voice starts to blurr and sound like a distant *whirrr*. It's not because you don't think what they are saying is important, but sometimes your brain just drifts off into space while they read to you or talk to you about your day. I've got the perfect stealth tool to keep your mind back here on Earth. This weighted fidget will keep your brain engaged and allow you to have some awesome conversations that you might otherwise be too spaced-out for.

## How to Make Ahead

Start by painting your nuts and letting them dry. This could take several coats of paint; be sure to let each coat dry before starting the next layer.

When your nuts are the desired color and dry, use a paintbrush to apply one layer of decoupage glue on the outside of each nut. This will make it harder for the color to get scratched off as you fidget.

## How to Use This Tool

This is the perfect activity for when you are feeling antsy and wiggly. It is great while you watch a movie, listen to a story or go for long car rides. Simply screw the nuts onto the bolt so that you have the colors in the order of a rainbow. This is a heavy fidget and should be used cautiously. The weight is great for calming your senses but can really hurt if it drops on your big toe.

## Challenge

Try to make a pattern with your nuts or try putting them on without looking.

Placing each nut on your fingers (like rings) can feel calming and soothing as well.

Can you stack your nuts on the table without them falling down?

## TRAIN YOUR ADULT ★

This nuts and bolts fidget is perfect because it is heavy, giving you both tactile (say: tak-til) and proprioceptive (say: proh-pree-uh-sep-tiv) input. You already know the brain-boosting benefits of fidgets (see page 69), but did you know that adding weight to your fidget adds an extra layer of calming strength to the tool? If you are a kid who runs at super-high speed, notice how the weight on your hands has an immediate calming and relaxing effect.

### What You Need

Acrylic paint (red, orange, yellow, green, blue, purple)

Paintbrush

Decoupage glue

6–10 hex nuts (any size will work; we used ⅝" [1.6 cm])

1 large bolt (same diameter as the hex nuts)

# SEATED SILLY BUSTERS

If you've ever had to wait for very long, you've probably been told by your adult to "settle down" or "quit wiggling." If they only knew how much your body needs those wiggles to help you understand your place in space. You can thank your proprioceptive (say: proh-pree-uh-sep-tiv) system for this. This doesn't mean you have to sit completely still; it just means you have to find stellar seated exercises to bust the sillies and get your adults on board. These seated exercises will give your brain just the boost it needs to keep you on track.

## How to Use This Tool

**Chair Push-Ups for a Quick Focus Booster:** While seated in your chair, put both of your hands on the sides of your seat and push down through your arms until your body rises from the chair. Try holding until the count of three before releasing. You can do this almost undetected by the adults sitting near you.

**Posture Check for a Speedy Attention Finder:** Simply sit straight up in your chair with your feet firmly on the ground. If you chair is too high, you might need to scoot to the end of the chair. Now, press your knees together and squeeze your bottom tightly to sit tall. Try to pull your belly button toward your spine (back). Keep your shoulders down and take in a few deep breaths. How long can you sit like this?

**Face Workouts to Clear Day-Dreaming:** While you are sitting at your seat, your body and mind can start to drift away. Take a minute to scrunch up your face as tightly as you can and then relax it again. Try to scrunch your eyebrows, eyes, lips and even your nose before letting go.

**Under-Table Tap Dance for a Boost of Energy:** When you start to get wiggly, try to move your feet with this easy exercise. Start in a seated position with just your toes resting on the ground. Reach one leg in front of you and tap your heel to the ground. Return your leg to starting position and do the next foot. Alternate your legs for 3 to 5 minutes.

## Challenge

There are so many other awesome exercises you can do while you are seated. If it is time to do spelling words, can you use your feet to do the movements to the letters of your words? How about trying to tap out your math problems with your toes? The possibilities are endless.

## What You Need

A chair, a bench, a car seat (anywhere you have to sit for a long period of time)

Your body

## TRAIN YOUR ADULT ★

These seated exercises will give your body the movement it needs while squashing your boredom. These are perfect for restaurants, the car or at your desk at school. If you are a kid who seems to crave constant movement, give your vestibular (say: ve-stib-yuh-ler) sense of movement the feedback it's looking for. Trust me, your brain will thank you by rewarding you with a great mood and a calm body. Remember, the key is to do them quietly so you are a stealthy secret agent and your adult sees how helpful they are!

# FINGER KNIT FASHION

Belts, scarves and bracelets . . . oh my! Boost your finger strength and bust boredom at the same time with these super Finger Knit Fashions. Make everyone in your family a fashionista while you wait. Not only will you keep your brain engaged, but you will be the talk of your friends because you will be creating something magical and special with your own hands. Finger knitting is an awesome boredom buster that can be taken anywhere you go. Grab your yarn and take it with you everywhere. You might even want to talk your grown-up into keeping a ball of yarn in the car so you can have something to keep your fingers busy anytime you need it. Think of this as your secret weapon against boredom: Throw a ball of yarn in your pocket and you are ready for any boring occasion.

## How to Use This Tool

Start by placing yarn between your thumb and pointer finger of the hand you use least, leaving a small tail (extra yarn) hanging down. Next, wrap the yarn behind your pointer finger and in front of your middle finger and then go behind the middle finger and back in front of your pointer finger. Think of a figure eight with your fingers inside. Do this two times. We like to call this part our fence.

Now you are ready to knit the yarn together. With your palm still facing you and starting with your pointer finger, pull the yarn on the bottom over the top piece to the back. (We say our sheep are jumping over the fence.) Do this for both fingers before making the figure eight again.

Repeat this process (build the fence, jump the sheep) over and over again to form a long rope. When you get to the desired length, pull the loop from your pointer finger to the loop on your middle finger and bring the bottom yarn over the top one last time. You will be left with one small loop. Cut your yarn so it has another long tail and thread the tail through the loop before pulling tight.

Once you have gotten the hang of finger knitting, you can make tons of items. Simply make long ropes and turn them into scarves, belts or jump ropes. You can make shorter ropes into bracelets, rings or even headbands. These long ropes make fantastic fidgets and calming tools as well as awesome crafts to share with friends.

## Challenge

Try using different textures and types of yarn to change the feeling and input you get from the finished product.

Try making the finger knit pattern with more than two fingers. This will make a thicker rope that is super fun to play with.

## TRAIN YOUR ADULT ★

It will be easy to get your grown-up on board with this activity when they see how busy it keeps your fingers and how quickly it calms you down. They might even be surprised to see your handwriting improve, because projects like this are perfect for strengthening the muscles in your hands and training your brain to follow multistep directions.

## What You Need
Yarn of any color and thickness

# COSMIC COMIC BOOK KIT

Superheroes to the rescue once again! With this take-along comic book kit, you will never have to wait for your next adventure to begin. Now you can take your adventures with you. This is the perfect boredom buster for long car rides and outings around town.

## How to Make Ahead

The only thing you need to do ahead of time is print off several copies of the Comic Book Page template (page 199) and a few copies of the Speech Bubble template (page 200). Take these and the other items on the supply list and pack them into your plastic case or a resealable plastic bag so they are easy to take with you anywhere. If you want to get fancy, you can decorate the case with stickers and your name.

## How to Use This Tool

Anytime you are in the mood to tell your super story, whip out your comic book kit and get to work. Think of your latest struggle and turn it into a comic adventure or use your world (the place you are waiting) as the setting for your story. The sky is the limit to the adventures you will create. The comic book template is perfect for drawing each of the parts of your story with your pencil and then coloring in with your colored pencils or markers. Add the words of your superhero using the text bubble template. Use the white paper when you are finished to make your cover, but don't forget to add your name to the cover as the author!

## TRAIN YOUR ADULT ★

Engaging your visual sense of sight, you can create the most elaborate adventure without leaving your seat. Think of how the stars of all the comic books you know have inner struggles and use their superpowers to do good things. How can you harness your superpowers with this fun take-along kit? Turning your struggles into the villain of the story can be invigorating and powerful as your hero (you) overcomes his or her biggest obstacles. Really struggling to solve a problem? Get your adult in on the action and have him or her add to your story to create the best adventure ever told.

## What You Need

Comic Book Page template (page 199)

Speech Bubble template (page 200)

Colored pencils and/or markers

Pencils/pens

White paper

Scissors

Plastic case (optional)

Stickers (optional)

# SHHH! NO-SEW QUIET BOOK

Most superkids love making noise. I get it, I promise. However, there are times when your adult will need you to be your absolute quietest self. Think of it like you are being super stealthy and secretive. You don't want anyone to detect your presence, or else! These SHHH! No-Sew Quiet Books will do just the trick at those times.

## How to Make Ahead

To make each of the pages of your book, you will need three felt pieces glued together when everything is finished. First, add glue to the first felt piece on all the edges and carefully lay another piece of felt on top. Next, add glue to the edges of the top piece on the stacked felt and carefully lay your last piece of felt on top. Set these to the side to dry. Repeat this process for the number of pages you need in the book.

For each game, we made the game on the right page and a blank page with pockets on the left. You can make the pockets by cutting a large rectangle out of felt and gluing half of it to the page. Add glue to the sides of this rectangle and fold it up to make a pocket.

Tic-Tac-Toe: Cut four thin strips of black felt and glue them in the shape of a tic-tac-toe board. Then use alternating colors to cut X and O pieces from felt. You can use felt letters for this but we liked the kid-made letters better.

Checkers: Cut 1-inch (2.5-cm) squares from any color felt (we used white). Place and glue these pieces on a page to make a checkerboard pattern. Using two more colors of felt, cut small circles for your game pieces.

Emotions: Cut out a face shape from skin-colored felt and glue to the middle of a page of felt. Use other colors of felt to make facial features such as eyes, nose, ears and hair. Using the feelings list on page 182, make different felt mouths to show a variety of emotions. Now, you can use your quiet book to expand your emotional recognition.

When all of your pages are complete, you can decorate the cover of your book with letters, shapes and designs. Using a hole punch, put holes along the left side of the book and fasten with ribbon.

## Challenge

There are so many fun games and patterns you can make for your quiet book. Here are three more ideas.

Spelling Practice: Cut two small lines from black felt and place sideways on your page to look like lines on a paper. Gather felt letters or your own letters cut from felt and put in a pocket on the facing page. Now you can make your spelling words using your letters inside the lines.

Tangrams: Cut out shapes (rectangles, squares and triangles) out of a variety of colors of felt. Use the blank page to create pictures using the shapes. Can you make a rocket, a house or a flower?

Roads & Tracks: Use gray felt to cut out long rectangles to use as tracks and roads for an on-the-go car track to use with your favorite miniature car set.

Can you think of other classic games that you'd like to take with you on your next trip? Othello, Memory, Tetris, I Spy . . . the possibilities are endless.

## TRAIN YOUR ADULT ★

This makes the perfect pack-and-play craft for busy kids! Not only is playing with this craft perfect for boosting your memory and increasing your focus, but creating the craft will work the tiny muscles in your hands, making your handwriting soar!

### Superpowers
hand strength, following directions, planning and prioritizing, critical thinking

### Sensory Systems
touch, sight

### Energy Scale
⚡⚡⚡⚡

### What You Need

Felt rectangles (we got ours at the dollar store)

Craft glue or hot glue

Felt letters (optional)

Ribbon

# COOL AS A CUCUMBER CALM-DOWN KIT

Not every day will be full of sunshine and rainbows. In fact, no matter how much awesome you possess, you will still find yourself at the brink of explosion some days. This Cool as a Cucumber Calm-Down Kit is just the tool you need when your heart starts to race, your palms get sweaty and you feel your control start to slip away. With this kit in hand, you will feel calm enough to face even your biggest fears and kick your most terrifying worries to the curb.

## How to Make Ahead

Only a few items need to be made ahead, which makes this super easy to put together. To start, get an adult to help you cut one pool noodle into 2-inch (5-cm) thick circles and place a few of these in your calm-down kit. Next, add a few drops of your favorite scent to a small piece of felt or fabric and add this to your kit. Finally, gather all your other materials, place them in your container and put your kit in a quiet and comfortable place in your house. If you are feeling crafty, decorate the outside with images and words that remind you of your happy place.

## How to Use This Tool

This kit is the perfect on-the-go calming tool when you are starting to get revved up with excitement or frustration. Each of the items in the kit encourages you to focus your senses and remove yourself from what is causing you to bubble up.

**Pool Noodle:** Squeeze one or two pool noodle circles in the palm of your hand to ease your fidgets or get your frustrations out.

**Felt:** Take a big deep breath, close your eyes and smell the scent on the fabric. This will engage your olfactory (say: ol-fak-tuh-ree) sense of smell and send calming juices straight to your brain.

**Pipe Cleaners:** These are great for soothing your nerves as you run your fingers down them or wrap them around your fingers. We like to make them into figure eights and use them as mini-fidgets.

**Balloons:** These are great for blowing up and letting out the air. If you struggle with taking big, deep breaths, these can help you!

**Large Pom-Poms:** These make the perfect fuzzy pets to squeeze between your fingers when you can't take your favorite stuffed animal with you.

**Straws:** Try blowing your pom-pom across the floor or across the table. Focusing your attention and using your oral motor skills will send calming signals to your brain and the rest of your body will follow.

## Challenge

There are so many things you can add to your Cool as a Cucumber Calm-Down Kit. Many items around the house such as your favorite maze book, a small pocket mirror and even a vibrating toothbrush can be calming. This book is full of calming tools as well: Calming Slime (page 135), Chill-Out Squish Balls (page 86), Rainbow Nuts and Bolts Fidget (page 73), Wizardly Worry Stones (page 32) and more.

## TRAIN YOUR ADULT ★

Grown-ups don't always know the right things to say or the right way to handle their superstars when they get upset, and, likewise, you might not know the best way to come back to zero when you feel an explosion starting to build. Learning to recognize these big feelings is called emotional regulation (say: ih-moh-shuh-nl reg-yuh-ley-shuhn), which is the most crucial skill any superstar can learn. Learning to recognize and regulate your emotions takes a lot of practice. Think of it like learning how to prevent a fire instead of how to escape one. Both skills are important, but avoiding a fire altogether is better for everyone.

**Superpowers**
emotional regulation, impulse control, problem solving, flexible thinking, self-regulation, self-calming

**Sensory Systems**
touch, sight, oral, body awareness

**Energy Scale**

## What You Need

Pool noodle

Calming scents (vanilla extract, lavender essential oil, cedar wood oil, etc.)

Felt

Pipe cleaners

Balloons

Large pom-poms

Straws

Plastic pencil case or shoebox

# MESMERIZING LEGO® MAZE

**Superpowers**
attention to detail, motor planning, hand strength, self-calming

**Sensory Systems**
sight

**Energy Scale**
⚡⚡⚡

Have you ever noticed your grown-ups rushing you to get ready to leave the house, only to make you wait for them to actually leave? Kick boredom to the curb when you create the coolest LEGO® maze on the block. Make them big, make them small, make them blue, make them green . . . it doesn't matter. The magic is in the creativity you use to construct your LEGO® maze. Now, the next time you are ready before the rest of the family, you can sit quietly and play with your maze and keep yourself out of the danger zone.

## How to Make Ahead

Starting with a large LEGO® baseplate, build a wall around the edges of the square with the long LEGO® pieces (we used 1x8), leaving two openings for the entrance and the exit of your maze. Next, use your long LEGO® pieces of different lengths to make a pathway at least 2 to 3 bricks wide, that goes from one opening to the other opening. You can make this as easy or as difficult as your imagination lets you.

## How to Use This Tool

Once you have built your maze, it is time for the best part: playing with your maze. Use your marble to try to get from one side of your maze to the other.

This maze is great for staying out of trouble while you wait for everyone else to get ready or while you run errands with your grown-up.

## Challenge

Can you make your maze resemble a letter in your name?

Can you make a mini version to keep in your Cool as a Cucumber Calm-Down Kit (page 82)?

Try adding multiple exits and putting several marbles through your maze at a time.

## What You Need

Large LEGO® baseplate

Long LEGO® pieces (1x2, 1x3, 1x4, etc.)

Marbles

## TRAIN YOUR ADULT ★

When grown-ups think of calming tools and strategies, they usually think of deep breaths (like on page 29) and stress balls (like on page 86). What many people don't know is that using your visual sense to focus on small objects, paths or problem solving can be extremely calming to the brain. Adding a LEGO® maze to your calm-down area is a great way to keep your mind busy and train your brain to focus on the maze while calming down to talk about your problems.

# CHILL-OUT SQUISH BALLS

Waiting can lead to busy little fingers. Busy little fingers can lead to frustrated adults. No worries! Chill out and squash those pesky nerves with these awesome squish balls. Even the most famous rock stars need to calm their nerves while waiting backstage. This simple squishy tool is easy to make but has huge benefits. You might be surprised just how much it calms your nerves. So much so, you might want to make one in every color.

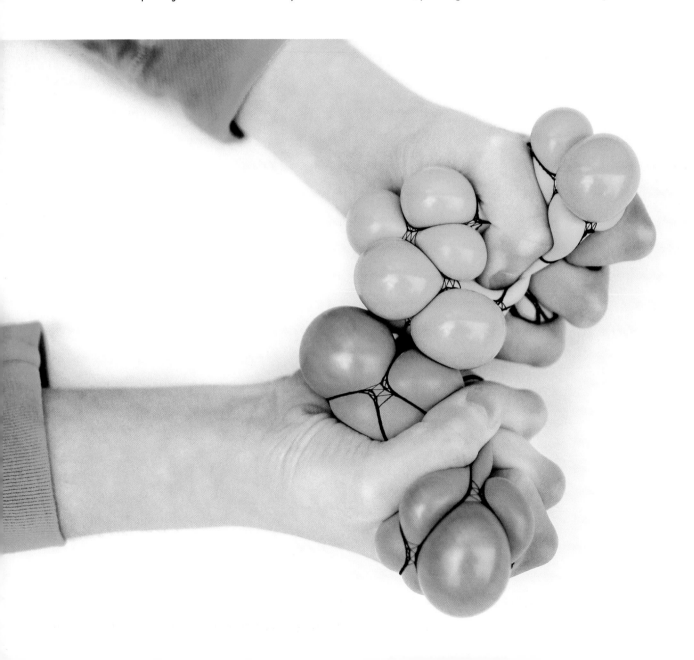

## How to Make Ahead

In a small bowl mix together the white glue, water and food coloring (if you are using it). After your mixture is evenly mixed, slowly pour in your liquid starch while stirring until your mixture becomes solid and pulls away from the bowl. This will make slime (learn more on page 135). Using a funnel, carefully pour your mixture into the empty plastic bottle and cover the opening of the bottle with the mouth of your balloon. This is the easiest way to get the slime into your balloon. Once you have poured most of your mixture into your balloon, carefully pull the balloon off the bottle and tie the balloon closed. Rinse off any slime that escaped the balloon and cover the balloon with the fishnet stockings. You will want to make sure you tie the rubber bands tight around the stockings so they don't break.

## How to Use This Tool

When you are feeling fidgety, frustrated or even just in need of some extra movement in your hands, grab a stress ball and squeeze away. Be sure to keep sharp objects and even your fingernails from the sides of the balloon or you will have a nasty mess on your hands (which is the opposite of calming).

## Challenge

Try making color-mixing calming stress balls. Make red slime and add it to a blue balloon. See what happens. What other colors can you mix?

Calming stress balls can be filled with many other items. Try the oobleck from page 143, playdough from page 106 or even something simple such as uncooked rice or dried beans.

## TRAIN YOUR ADULT ★

If your adult is nervous about giving you a ball when your nerves are rattled, remind them just how much these give your little fingers the push back they need using your proprioceptive sense of body awareness and how much they will tingle your tactile sense of touch. By squeezing the squish ball, the nerves in your hand will be supercharged, sending calming chemicals, a.k.a. endorphins (say: en-dawr-fins), to your brain. Amazing that such a simple craft reduces stress and wakes up your brain to help you rock your day!

### Superpowers
hand strength, emotional regulation, self-calming, self-monitoring, impulse control, concentration, focus

### Sensory Systems
touch, body awareness, sight

### Energy Scale
⚡⚡⚡⚡

### What You Need

½ cup (120 ml) white glue

½ cup (120 ml) water

Food coloring (optional)

½ cup (120 ml) liquid starch

Empty plastic bottle

Balloons

Fishnet stockings

Small rubber bands

# TO THE MOON COUNTDOWN BANNER

**Superpowers**
patience, flexible thinking, impulse control, planning and prioritizing, self-monitoring, time management, communication

**Sensory Systems**
sight

**Energy Scale**
⚡⚡

Three, two, one . . . Blastoff! Every rocket engineer knows how important a good countdown is. That doesn't stop him or her from getting anxious (say: angk-shuhs) before the big day. A secret tip to simmering that anxiety is to create a visual countdown. This countdown banner is perfect to create before you launch into your next big adventure! Long car rides . . . count the hours. Starting school in a few days . . . count the days. No matter how big your adventure, this countdown banner will ease your worries and help you blast off to success.

## How to Make Ahead

Start by drawing a large rocket on your white paper (you want it to be the size of the entire paper) and coloring it in to your liking. Next, use your red, orange and yellow paper or felt to cut out flames. On each flame write a number from 1 to 5 (or higher if you have more time to wait for your big launch). Once your flames and rocket have been made, attach your ribbon to the back of your rocket using glue. You want a tail hanging down from the rocket long enough to hold all your flames. Using the clothespins, attach your flames to the ribbon in order from 1 to 5 under your rocket. You are ready to count down!

## How to Use This Tool

Anytime you are nearing a big transition (say: tran-zish-uhn)—a change in plans or events in your life—you can set the rocket up with the amount of flames you need to represent the number of days, hours or minutes you have to wait. Remove one flame at a time until it is time to blast off!

## Challenge

This rocket countdown can be large or small. Try to make a pocket edition or one small enough to go in a car with you to count down your hours.

## What You Need

Cardstock paper (white, red, orange, yellow)

Felt (optional)

Markers

Ribbon (1" [2.5 cm] wide)

Glue

Clothespins

## TRAIN YOUR ADULT ★

Transitions can be the most dreaded part of any grown-up's day. They know these times of day are tough but they don't know how to make them smoother. Visual timers and countdowns help your brain recognize the passing of time in a concrete way and give you a clear understanding of the sequence of events that need to take place. If you struggle to move from one activity to another without a bad attitude, adding a visual countdown could be just what you and your grown-up need to smooth out frustrations.

# CHAPTER 4

# STELLAR LEARNING SECRETS TO MAKE YOU A ROCK-STAR LEARNER

Even the most awesome superheroes have to train and learn the basics to save the world. You are no exception! That doesn't mean that learning can't be fun and you can't harness your need to wiggle and move to do great things. These activities and crafts will help you be awesome at school, during homework or while learning new things. From rock-star memory boosters to fabulous fidget fixes, these activities will give you more focus and increased attention and will help you get ready for a terrific learning day!

From memorizing facts to sitting still long enough to do your homework, this can be the biggest source of arguments and battles with your grown-ups. The secret to rocking your learning and knocking it out of the park each and every time is to clear your mind before you ever get started and take frequent brain breaks. Having a clear head will let you think about your tasks and get started right away, while brain breaks will give your body and brain the boost they need to keep going. It is totally normal to get a cloudy brain any time you put it to the test. Don't hesitate to remind your grown-up when you need a break. In our home, we like to take breaks every fifteen minutes. But I will be honest . . . as mom, I need my superkids to remind me exactly what their brains and bodies need. You can remind your grown-ups too!

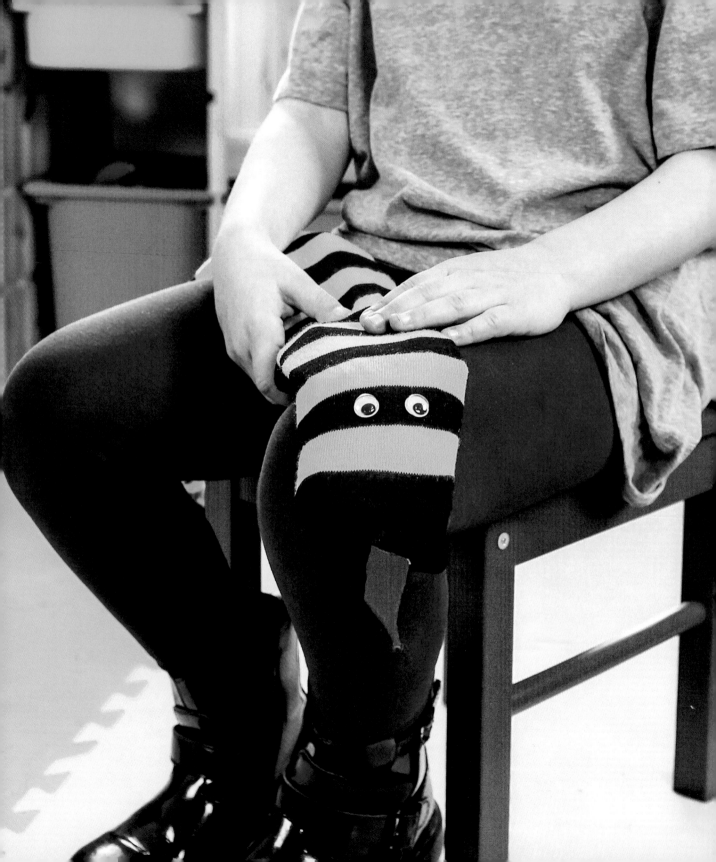

# WEIGHTED SNAKE LAP BUDDIES

Master the art of snake charming without handling real, live snakes. With these fantastic weighted lap buddies, you will be charming more than just snakes. If you ever struggle with adults telling you to sit still, quit wiggling or pay attention, you will definitely want to make a few of these. Your adults will be charmed and mesmerized by your instant focus and calm when you whip out your snake buddy.

## How to Make Ahead

Start by lining up your resealable plastic bags on top of your knee-high sock in a straight line. You should have enough sock left after your line of bags for room to tie the end. (This was four bags for us.) Fill your resealable plastic bags with equal amounts of rice. Before you close your bags, push all the air out of the bags and lay them flat. Use duct tape to connect each of the bags of rice together in a line (it should look like a train) and then cover all of the bags with one layer of tape for more protection. Set these to the side until you are done making your snake.

Using fabric glue or hot glue, attach two wiggly eyes to the toe of the sock. Cut a small rectangular shape from the red felt and then cut a triangle out of the tip to make it look like a snake tongue. Next, use glue to attach the tongue to the very end of the sock's toe.

Once your sock snake is dry, insert your taped bags into the sock, tie the opening of the sock to make the rattle and close up the lap snake.

## How to Use This Tool

Your weighted snake is perfect for on the go, around the house or at school. Anytime you are feeling a little antsy or full of movement when you need to be seated, pull out your weighted buddy and throw him over your lap.

## TRAIN YOUR ADULT ★

Did you know that when you place pressure on your joints, your body gets proprioceptive (say: proh-pree-uh-sep-tiv) input that calms it? You've probably already noticed that you can be easily distracted by the sensory input around you (chairs moving, fans whirring, lights flickering, etc.). What your brain needs is a physical reminder to ground it and refocus attention on the work in front of you. When you add pressure, your brain increases endorphin (happy-hormone) levels and decreases heart rate and blood pressure (from increased stress). If you are a kiddo who seeks out pressure, you will love having this buddy on your lap.

## What You Need

Quart-size (950-ml) resealable plastic bags

Knee-high socks

Dry uncooked rice

Duct tape

Fabric glue or hot glue

Wiggly eyes

Red felt

# SUPERSONIC LISTENING PHONE

If you've ever wished for supersonic hearing and focus, look no further. This listening phone will triple your hearing and hone your listening skills anytime you use it! If you've ever read a story out loud and then immediately forgotten it, or you've sat in a class and felt completely distracted by all the chairs moving, papers crumpling or pencils sharpening, this is the tool for you! This supersonic listening phone is the answer to better reading comprehension as it tunes out the distractions around you. Plus, it looks super cool!

## How to Make Ahead
Have an adult cut your long PVC pipe down to 6 inches (15 cm). Next, put your pieces together so that your pipe is in the shape of a letter C. Now you can paint your pieces with acrylic paint in any design you desire. This might take several coats of paint. If so, let each coat dry completely before adding a new coat of paint. When your paint is dry, you can add a coat of decoupage glue to seal your paint and keep it from chipping or scratching.

## How to Use This Tool
The next time you are reading your favorite book, working on spelling words or reading directions to finish a project, use your listening phone to speak into. Your voice will be amplified and all the other distractions in the room will seem to fade away. The best part is you will be the only one who can hear your super-strength voice, as the listening phone directs your voice back to your own ear!

## Challenge
This listening phone is great for hearing individual sounds in words. Try a game where you break your spelling words into small parts while saying them into your listening phone. How many parts do you hear? What letter sounds do you hear?

## TRAIN YOUR ADULT ★

Help your grown-up help you by reminding them you need this tool to fine-tune your listening skills. Now you will be able to harness the power of your auditory (say: aw-di-tawr-ee) sense of hearing to block out all the outside noises and distractions while you read. Many superkids (and even grown-ups) learn best when they read out loud or repeat what they are learning. This tool allows you to do just that without distracting others around you while at the same time making your voice stand out against the noises you are surrounded by.

## What You Need
PVC pipe pieces: 2 (90°) corners, 1 (45°) corner, 1 long pipe

Handsaw (with adult help)

Acrylic paint

Paintbrush

Decoupage glue

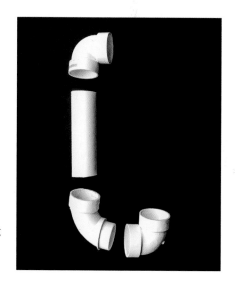

# SPELLBOUND JELL-O® JIGGLERS

**Superpowers**
hand strength, working memory, following directions

**Sensory Systems**
taste, touch, sight

**Energy Scale**
♪♪♪♪

No wizard is complete without his or her book of spells. Spelling book, that is. Not all wizards can remember their spelling words and spells with ease. These tasty spellbound jigglers will have your memory working in no time and will mystify your adults when they hear that you want to practice your spelling words.

Note: This recipe makes six large alphabet gummies. We made a batch for each color of the rainbow by using this recipe six times and changing the Jell-O® flavors and colors each time.

## How to Make Ahead

Start with extremely cold water and stir in your corn syrup until it is dissolved. With adult supervision, pour your mixture into a saucepan on the stove and add in the gelatin and Jell-O® packs. Cook on medium heat for 5 minutes, continuously stirring until the mixture is completely liquefied. Next, have your grown-up carefully pour your mixture into a heat-resistant glass and let it sit for 5 minutes. Once all the foam has risen to the top, you can scrape it off and begin pouring the syrup into your molds.

Fill your molds to the top and let them sit on the counter for at least 5 hours or until firm. Carefully remove your alphabet jigglers and get ready to cast a "spell."

## How to Use This Tool

Once you have your patch of alphabet jigglers, you can spell any word you want. Try to make your name, sight words or even words that are usually very tricky. What words can you spell with this delicious treat?

## TRAIN YOUR ADULT ★

Learning to spell can be boring and repetitive. Sometimes grown-ups feel lost trying to help you learn your words without becoming a bore. Also, remembering how words are spelled can be extra difficult for some superkid wizards. That's okay, it just means your working memory (the function of the brain the helps you remember facts) needs a little wizardly practice. These gummies are a yummy and fun way to get lots of practice! Encourage your adults to keep a batch handy for your next spelling list that comes home from school. For more fun games to boost your working memory, check out Squishy Sight Words (page 101), Addition Stomp (page 103) and Super Stretchy Spelling Words (page 117).

## What You Need

½ cup (120 ml) cold water

¼ cup (60 ml) corn syrup

2 (4-oz [113-g]) packs unflavored gelatin

1 (5-oz [141-g]) pack Jell-O®

Alphabet candy mold

# DIY CHEWABLE JEWELRY

Do the ends of your pencils look like a wild animal was let loose on them? Maybe your fingernails look like they've been through a blender? In fact, have you noticed that anytime you sit to focus, your fingers, sleeves or pencils go straight to your mouth? That's because chewing has been proven to increase focus, and your body is just doing its job! Harness that need to chew into a healthy and socially acceptable alternative with this stylish chewable. When you give in to the need to chew, your brain will reward you by increasing your focus and reducing the anxiety that might keep you from otherwise completing your schoolwork.

## How to Make Ahead

Start by cutting off the bottom (the hem) and the top (from the underarms up) of your shirt. You will be left with the middle (belly) of your shirt. Take this part of your shirt and cut it into 1-inch (2.5-cm) pieces, cutting across your shirt. You don't have to be perfectly straight; just do your best. This will make rings of T-shirt material. Gently stretch your loops and save two loops for later.

Once you have all of your rings the same size, gather them together. Cut your extra two rings into long strips and use them to wrap around the collection of rings at the top. This will make a band to hold them all in place. Tie your extra strips together tightly and trim the tails.

## How to Use This Tool

Once you have created your necklace, you are ready to wear your new fashion. The next time you have the urge to chew away at your shirt, you can gnaw on your new necklace. Go ahead and throw it in the wash with the rest of your laundry at the end of the day, so it is ready for a new day!

## Challenge

You can make your necklace as wide or as small as you wish. If you want a smaller necklace, use fewer loops or a smaller shirt.

Try braiding the strips, if you like a less "messy" looking necklace.

Try using a baby shirt to make a bracelet.

## TRAIN YOUR ADULT ★

Science tells us that chewing things (such as gum) actually helps us concentrate and retain information. By increasing blood flow to the part of the brain that controls focus and providing proprioceptive (say: proh-pree-uh-sep-tiv) input to the jaw, chewing will give your brain the boost it needs to react faster and do better on tests. So the next time your grown-up tells you to stop gnawing, remind them the real answer is to give you an awesome alternative to harness your intense need to chew. The results will keep everyone happy.

**Superpowers**
self-regulation, impulse control, self-awareness

**Sensory Systems**
oral, touch, body awareness

**Energy Scale**
⚡⚡⚡

## What You Need

Old T-shirt

Scissors

# SQUISHY SIGHT WORDS

Taking over the world takes big plans. Those big plans require lots of reading and writing. What better way to sharpen your reading and writing skills than to master as many sight words (words that your brain automatically remembers) as you possibly can. Your brain is working overtime to be totally awesome, and you want to take the load off as much as possible. By practicing your sight words on this super galactic squish pad, you will ingrain the words in your memory bank and use your super sensory powers to fine-tune your handwriting at the same time.

## How to Make Ahead
Start by filling your resealable plastic bag with a bottle of clear hair gel, a few drops of food coloring and glitter. Slowly push the air out of your bag but be careful not to let the hair gel squeeze out of the bag. Close your resealable plastic bag completely. Next, add duct tape to all four sides of your bag and fold the tape over so it covers both sides of the bag. It should look like a frame. Write your sight words on index cards and you are ready to go!

## How to Use This Tool
Pull one index card, say the word, spell the word and then turn your card over. Now write your word on your sight-word frame using your finger (anything sharp could puncture the bag). Once you have written your word, check your work.

## Challenge
Try to make sentences or silly stories using the sight words you are working on.

Can you use this squishy bag for your math practice by writing your math facts?

Younger children can use this to practice writing their name or drawing their shapes.

## What You Need
1-gallon (3.8-L) resealable plastic bag

6 oz (180 ml) clear hair gel

Food coloring

Glitter

Duct tape

Pen

Index cards

## TRAIN YOUR ADULT ★

Did you know that your brain is divided into different regions that process information from your world (sounds, sights, emotions, etc.) one at a time? Before these sections of your brain can talk to one another, they have their own processes they have to finish. When we engage more than one sense at a time (like seeing and writing) our brain works faster and more efficiently, building links between information and boosting memory skills. The next time your grown-up asks you to memorize words, get your fingers ready for some tactile work to boost your memory bank.

# ADDITION STOMP

Do you dread doing your math facts and homework? Do you forget what 9+7 is and want to hide when the math worksheets come out? Don't fret. Turn into Godzilla with this loud and crushing game. Now you can work on your facts and harness your inner need to smash and crash at the same time!

## How to Make Ahead

Start by writing the numbers 0 through 9 on each of the white paper bags with your marker. Fill each bag with 1 or 2 plastic grocery bags and set the numbers on a hard floor surface in order.

## How to Use This Tool

There are two ways to play this game. If you know your math facts and are just in need of a little memory practice, you will try to jump on both numbers at the same time while saying the answers. So if your problem is 5+3, you will stomp on the 5 bag and 3 bag at the same time while shouting 8.

If math is new to you or you need to count up to find your answer, you will start with the number in your head and then stomp on one bag for each number as you count up. For example, using 5+3, you would say 5 in your head and then stomp on 1, 2 and 3 bags as you count up 6, 7, 8.

## Challenge

Try harder problems that involve double digits by making more bags.

Try using these for multiplication by stomping on the numbers and shouting the answers.

Make a set of alphabet bags and stomp your name or spelling words.

## TRAIN YOUR ADULT ★

Learning does not mean you have to sit in a seat all day, look at the teacher and be quiet. In fact, science tells us that our brains remember things much better if we move, stomp and wiggle as we work. Getting your body moving is just what your brain needs to help you remember all the facts being thrown at you. Using your auditory (say: aw-di-tawr-ee) sense of hearing and your proprioceptive (say: proh-pree-uh-sep-tiv) sense of body awareness, your brain will make connections to the math facts. If your grown-up is skeptical, just tell them you are building your working memory and using your proprioceptive (say: proh-pree-uh-sep-tiv) sense of body awareness to ingrain these facts to memory!

**Superpowers**
working memory, problem solving, focus, concentration, alertness, self-awareness

**Sensory Systems**
sight, body awareness, movement

**Energy Scale**

## What You Need

10 white paper bags

Marker

Recycled plastic grocery bags

Index cards (optional)

# GALAXY HANDWRITING SAND TRAY

Have you ever tried to read a treasure map or instructions your friend scribbled down for you but couldn't make heads or tails of the information because it looked more like abstract art than handwriting? Unfortunately, that is often how adults feel when they try to read your handwriting. What they don't know is handwriting is boring. Not only will this galaxy tray build muscle memory, but it will boost your hand strength and reinforce the proper letter formation without ever having to pick up a pencil.

## How to Make Ahead

Start by covering the bottom of a black tray with a layer of aluminum foil. Next, pour in enough black sand to cover the bottom of the tray. Add in the blue and purple sand and use your finger to add galactic swirls to the sand. Sprinkle a few stars onto the sand until you are pleased with your galaxy.

## How to Use This Tool

The next time you want to hone your handwriting skills, grab your galaxy tray and practice writing in the tray instead of on paper. As you run your fingers through your sand, you should start to see your lines and shapes shine through. Pay close attention to the direction you are moving your fingers and try to form your letters using "just right" letter formation. Remember, start at the top, go to the bottom and try to keep your finger in the sand without lifting it except when you absolutely have to. This will help you when you have to write your letters on paper using lines.

If the sand bothers your fingertips, you can use a chopstick to write in the sand, just be careful not to scratch your aluminum-foil base. Not only will it have the same effect as writing with your finger, but it will also give you practice holding your writing utensil correctly (without all the boring reminders from your grown-up).

## Challenge

Have your adult draw a shape, word or number in the sand and try to match their writing.

Try writing your sight words or your name.

## TRAIN YOUR ADULT ★

Something really cool happens in your brain when you practice a skill repeatedly in fun and exciting ways. Much like never forgetting how to ride a bike once you've mastered it, the same can be said for writing your letters and sight words. In fact, did you know that one part of your brain, the cerebellum (say: ser-eh-bell-um) is mostly responsible for regulating your muscle memory? Science has proven that through repeated practice and sensory input, your brain works to commit these movements to memory, and they become second nature. The next time your grown-up wants you to practice something, remember they are helping you train your brain.

**Superpowers**
hand strength, working memory, attention to detail, concentration, focus

**Sensory Systems**
touch, sight

**Energy Scale**

**What You Need**
Black tray
Aluminum foil
Black sand
Blue sand
Purple sand
Glitter stars
Chopsticks (optional)

# 2-INGREDIENT FOCUS DOUGH

Sitting to do schoolwork can be so boring. Yawn! What if I told you I have a secret playdough you can make that will get you focused on your schoolwork and leave the adults staring in amazement at how you did it? This super simple dough is perfect for school, home or those times adults tell you to "calm down and focus." In fact, it is so effective at focusing your attention, your friends are going to want some too so they can be just as focused as you.

## How to Make Ahead

Measure the conditioner and the cornstarch in a small bowl and stir with a fork or mix together with your fingers. Next, squeeze the dough until it is soft and smooth and mixed evenly.

Finally, store the dough in a plastic bag for later use during your seated focused work.

Changing the measurements of the ingredients will change the look and feel of the dough. For a more slimy dough, use more conditioner. For a harder and firmer dough, use more cornstarch.

TIP: If you want to color your dough like we did, add a few drops of food coloring to the conditioner before mixing with the cornstarch.

## How to Use This Tool

This is definitely a "make-ahead" activity. It is super messy but uber fun. Once it is mixed, it becomes a delicious-smelling smooth playdough that isn't very messy at all.

Take a study break for 5 minutes and roll the playdough between your fingers. During a quiet activity such as reading or lecture time, squeeze and roll the dough between your fingers while you keep your eyes on the adult. Before you get started with your homework, take 5 to 10 minutes to boost your brain power and engage your senses by rolling your dough and pushing the dough with your fingertips.

## Challenge

Try using the dough to make your sight words, vocabulary words or even this week's spelling words. Hide some marbles in your dough to really challenge your brain and your visual skills. Can you find all the marbles you hid? What else could you hide?

## TRAIN YOUR ADULT ★

You might be wondering how playdough can be so powerful. When you sit for a long time, your body gets used to everything going on around you, then your mind wanders and your body wiggles. But when you touch the playdough, your tactile (say: tak-til) system tells your brain to wake up and pay attention. As you squeeze the playdough, your proprioceptive (say: proh-pree-uh-sep-tiv) system (your body's way of making sense of pressure on your joints and muscles) tells your brain, "Hey, you, I'm here . . . pay attention."

**Superpowers**
Concentration, focus, hand strength, self-awareness

**Sensory Systems**
touch, smell, body awareness

**Energy Scale**
♪ ♪ ♪

## What You Need

1 cup (240 ml) scented conditioner

2 cups (225 g) cornstarch

Small plastic bag for storage

Food coloring (optional)

# SUPER FEELINGS BOOKMARKS

Have you ever felt like you were going to explode from anger or frustration? You are not alone. In fact, it is really hard for even the most controlled superhero to regulate emotions and make positive choices when his or her blood is boiling. With these bookmarks, you will have awesome choices at your fingertips for the next time you feel like you are going to explode and can't think straight. Simply take a peek at your bookmark and pick a calm-down tool to get you back to learning in no time at all.

## How to Make Ahead

Start by copying or tearing out the feelings bookmarks on page 195. Cut along the edge of the bookmarks and use your hole punch to put a hole in the top. Tie a small ribbon through the hole to make a tail. If you want your bookmarks to be sturdier, cover the front and back with clear tape and trim off the extra tape.

## How to Use This Tool

Keep these bookmarks handy and ready for when your super moods take over and you need help making choices that have positive consequences. The feelings bookmarks on page 195 are already made for the two most common emotions that get in the way of your learning (sad and angry). When you are feeling one of these emotions and can't calm yourself down, take a quick peek and find a strategy that will calm you down and get you back on track lickety-split.

## Challenge

Do you have other strategies that work well for you or other moods that keep you from learning? Add your own choices to the blank feelings bookmarks on page 196. Use this same idea to make a poster to hang in your room or calm-down space to help you remember exactly what options you have when you start to get sad, mad or scared. Use the feelings chart on page 182 for ideas to get you started.

## What You Need

Feelings Bookmarks (page 195)

Scissors

Hole punch

Ribbon

Clear tape (optional)

## TRAIN YOUR ADULT ★

Most people don't know that when we experience big emotions, our brain becomes disconnected, sending us into something called the fight, flight or freeze response. There is a reason you can't think of good calm-down options when you are upset. Your brain is in crisis mode and can't think logically. These bookmarks are full of simple ideas to help calm your brain and bring you back to a place where you can make good decisions. Use them to help communicate to the adults in your life what you need in your roughest moments.

# DIY DUCT TAPE WIGGLE SEAT

Sitting is for adults. Wiggling is for kids. Okay, that's not really how it works in the real world, but wouldn't it be nice? Now you can have the best of both worlds with a wiggle seat made entirely out of duct tape. Warning: All your friends will want one of these terrific tools too! Not only will this seat make you the coolest kid in your class, but it will make adults happy with the way it calms your body and focuses your brain during worktime.

## How to Make Ahead

The first thing you need to do is make two duct-tape sheets. Do this by laying 18 inches (45 cm) of duct tape faceup on your workspace. Then lay another 18-inch (45-cm) piece above this piece, overlapping just a little. Continue doing this until you have a square of tape 18 x 18 inches (45 x 45 cm). Starting at the base of your tape, lay a piece of 18-inch (45-cm) tape on top of your tape facedown. (This will cover the sticky part.) Do this all the way to the top of your sheet. Once you have this sheet complete, set it to the side and repeat this entire process.

Next, trim your tape sheets down to 16 x 16 inches (40 x 40 cm) so you have straight edges and clean lines. Lay both sheets on top of each other and tape three of the sides together using more duct tape. Leave one side completely untaped.

Place your pillow insert into the pocket you just made and close up the hole with one more strip of duct tape.

## How to Use This Tool

Take this wiggle seat anywhere you struggle to keep your bottom on the seat. While this seat is perfect for boosting focus when learning is crucial, this seat could be used anywhere . . . at the dinner table, in your school desk or even at a restaurant. At first glance, it will look like you are completely still, but your body will be getting the movement and wiggling it needs. Fool your grown-ups by using the seat to push against your bottom, rocking back and forth or rock back and forth without tipping your seat backward. You will be surprised how little your wiggles need to be to get the movement your body is asking for.

## What You Need

Duct tape

14 x 14" (35 x 35-cm) pillow insert

## TRAIN YOUR ADULT ★

When we wiggle, it is our way of finding our place in space. This is because of our proprioceptive (say: proh-pree-uh-sep-tiv) sense of body awareness. One super rad way to give your proprioceptive (say: proh-pree-uh-sep-tiv) system a push back is to make this fun wiggle seat! Show your grown-ups that wiggling isn't such a bad thing, as long as you have an easy-to-use boundary to keep you from falling out of your chair or disturbing the person next to you. This wiggle seat will send "just right" signals to your brain to keep you engaged in your learning and keep your energy in check.

# WHAT'S NEXT? VELCRO TASK CHART

Adults love to tell you what to do. Do this, then this, now this. While they have the best intentions, it can make even the most amazing ninja go crazy. The answer to getting everything done and staying calm is a simple task chart. If you've ever struggled to keep your desk organized, finish your schoolwork without getting distracted or complete your homework without getting frustrated, this is going to rock your world. By breaking your tasks into smaller parts, this stellar chart will keep your tasks in order and help you continue being the super ninja you are!

## How to Make Ahead

Start by folding the bottom half of your paper lengthwise toward the top almost halfway. This means you will have a little bit of the cardstock poking above the bottom half. Next, divide the smaller section into 6 equal 2-inch (5-cm) parts by drawing a line and cutting these pieces to the middle of your paper. You will be folding these back up toward the top.

Next, tear out or copy the tasks from page 193 and add the tasks you will be working on to your 6 sections on the larger part of the paper. Glue the titles to the tasks on the bottom flap and "Done" on the outside of the flaps when the flaps are folded up.

Finally, add Velcro to both the flaps and the larger section so that the flaps remain closed.

## How to Use This Tool

The next time you need to complete a task or have a list of projects to complete, try using a What's Next? Velcro Task Chart to break everything down into smaller parts.

Example breakdown for after school: Hang backpack, Eat snack, Read book, Brain break, Homework, Clean up supplies.

Start with all the flaps open. As you complete each task, fold up the section so that all you see is Done. Once all your flaps are closed, you know you can move on to another project.

## Challenge

This chart doesn't just have to be used for after school. Think about other parts of the day that could be shown on a task chart. You could make one for your chores, bedtime routine, the steps to cleaning your room, etc.

You can laminate or cover your task cards with clear tape to make them more durable. Add Velcro to the back of each card and on the chart so you can change your tasks and use your chart for many parts of your day.

## TRAIN YOUR ADULT ★

Executive functioning (say: ig-zek-yuh-tiv fuhngk-shuhning) is your brain's automatic to-do list. Sometimes it's hard for your brain to organize all the things you need to do, and you need some help to put the steps in order and help you remember what is next. I bet your adults use lists to help them remember what they need to get finished on time. Adults think in big projects, but superkids needs things broken down into smaller steps to ensure success. So the next time your grown-up tells you to finish your homework, ask him or her to break down the parts of your homework you need to do and add in breaks for brain-boosting snacks and movement.

---

**Superpowers**
motor planning, organization, decision making, working memory, time management, self-monitoring

**Sensory Systems**
sight

**Energy Scale**

---

**What You Need**

Cardstock paper (measuring 6 x 12" [16 x 30 cm])

What's Next? Task Cards (page 193)

Glue

Velcro dots

# SUPER SIMPLE SUPERHERO BRAIN BREAKS

Even superheroes have to train to stay faster than a speeding bullet and stronger than 300 men. Training isn't just for the muscles, either. In fact, you need to train your brain. Did you know that taking breaks from your work can actually train your brain to help you get your work done faster and help you concentrate better? Yeah, it's really cool science for superheroes like yourself.

## How to Use This Tool

Here are some super fun movement breaks when you need them. These brain breaks are the perfect excuse to get up from the table during homework or take a pause during reading. When you start to notice your mind wandering or your brain getting fuzzy, ask your adult to do some fun brain breaks with you to get you back on track and in the thinking game.

**Super Strength:** Flex both arm muscles and twist at the waist 10 times.

**X-ray Vision:** Squint your eyes and relax. Do this 15 times.

**Stealth Speed:** Run in place for 30 seconds.

**Super Leaps:** Squat down to the ground and then jump up with one fist in the air 6 times.

**Galactic Punch:** Alternate hands and punch the air with your fists. Do this 15 times.

**Wall Crawls:** Use your hands and feet to pretend to climb a wall for 60 seconds.

**Flying Power:** Lie on the floor on your belly and lift your feet and arms for 20 seconds.

**Mr. Elastic:** Bend your body forward, backward and sideways. Try to bend into 10 different positions.

## Challenge

This is just the beginning. What other superpowers and simple movements can you mimic while you take a break from thinking?

## TRAIN YOUR ADULT ★

A brain break doesn't involve taking a rest or snoozing away your time. It uses your body (through exercise) to give your brain a rest, while at the same time getting it geared up for more focus and attention. Your grown-up might think you are making things up when you tell them you need a moment to stop working and start moving, but after they see just how centered and focused you are afterward, they will be adding brain breaks to your learning routines more and more. Not only do these quick exercises increase your endurance, range of motion and coordination, but they increase the oxygen being sent to your brain.

**Superpowers**
focus, strength, coordination, flexibility, concentration, self-regulation

**Sensory Systems**
movement, body awareness

**Energy Scale**
⚡⚡⚡⚡⚡⚡⚡

## What You Need
Your body

# SUPER STRETCHY SPELLING WORDS

One of the best parts of being a kid is getting to move, twist and turn your body in all directions. What if I told you that you could use that movement to increase your memory and have fun while you do it? Turn into Captain Elastico with these Super Stretchy Spelling Words and build your working memory (your mental sticky notes) and long-term memory by making your spelling words with your body. The next time you have to remember how to spell something, you will automatically get a mental image of you bending and twisting your body into shape.

## How to Use This Tool

This activity is as simple as it sounds. The next time you have spelling words to practice or sight words to memorize, put the pencil down and head to open space so you have room to move your body. Bend your body to make the letters of your words. For example, if you are spelling the word *the*, you would turn your body into the letter *T* by putting your hands out to the side and standing up straight. Then you would turn into the letter *H* by putting both hands in the air and spreading your feet apart. Finally, you might sit on the floor with your feet in front of you and both hands stretched out for the other lines in the *E*.

## Challenge

If you have a digital camera, try getting someone to take pictures of you making different letters with your body. Print the pictures and make new words using your letter pictures.

Gather together a few friends and try making a string of letters to spell entire words or sentences.

## TRAIN YOUR ADULT ★

Are you a superkid who is always on the move? Keeping you in one place long enough to practice your sight words is probably a huge battle for your grown-up. Not anymore. By inverting your head, twisting your body and crossing the middle of your body (your midline), you will make connections in your brain you could never ever make with just a pencil and paper. As you move and stretch, your brain will connect these movements to the letters in your spelling words and build your body and your brain at the same time.

## What You Need

Your body

# SPLATTER PAINT MULTIPLICATION

**Superpowers**
attention to detail, working memory, problem solving, motor planning, hand strength, coordination

**Sensory Systems**
sight, movement, touch

**Energy Scale**
ℱ ℱ ℱ ℱ ℱ ℱ

Don't let the thought of numbers scare you. Instead, turn your dread of math practice into some super messy, super spectacular art with this awesome game that is perfect for adventure seekers. Practice your aim and make a splash while working on your math facts. By using your entire body and tons of sensory systems, you will make connections in your brain that will commit those facts to memory and put you ahead of the rest of the class!

## How to Make Ahead

Start by filling your balloons with paint. Fill your dropper with paint and carefully squeeze into your balloons. Clean off the mouth of your balloon, blow up the balloon and tie it off. Set aside for later. Repeat this until you have enough balloons to cover your large canvas. Next, tape your balloons onto your canvas. You can do this in rows or mixed up and scattered. Finally, with your permanent marker, write math facts you are working on right now on the ends of the balloons so you can see them from far away.

NOTE: You can't fill your balloons up too far in advance or the paint will dry out. If you need to set this up days in advance, add a little water to your balloon before you close it up.

## How to Use This Tool

Once you have your canvas set up, you are ready to create math art! You can do this with your friends or by yourself. Place your canvas of balloons against a wall or a tree and stand a good distance away from the canvas. Find a math problem you want to solve and say it out loud.

Throw your dart at the math problem and answer the problem it lands on (it's okay if it lands on a different problem than you claimed . . . aiming is hard). Once you have answered all the problems and broken all the balloons, carefully remove the leftover balloon parts and let your art dry. You can load the same canvas again for another round or start fresh. Your choice.

## Challenge

Don't just use this for multiplication. Use this fun art project for any facts you need to commit to memory. For younger superkids, this can be letter matching or counting. For older kids, this can be vocabulary words or difficult math problems.

## What You Need

Balloons

Droppers

Tempera paint

Tape

Large white canvas or poster board

Permanent marker

Darts

## TRAIN YOUR ADULT ★

Science tells us that when information enters the brain, more can be processed at one time when the information is spread between multiple senses. In fact, using your vestibular (say: ve-stib-yuh-ler), auditory (say: aw-di-tawr-ee) and visual (say: vizh-oo-uhl) senses will actually make it easier for your brain to commit these facts to your short-term memory and build your long-term lasting memory. Remind your adult that using your entire body connects wires in your brain and makes it easier for facts to find their way to a safe place in your memory banks.

# WEIGHTED MONSTER WALKING BUDDIES

**Superpowers**
self-regulation, impulse control, strength, self-awareness, self-monitoring, motor planning

**Sensory Systems**
body awareness, movement, touch

**Energy Scale**
♪♪♪

Don't touch that. Slow down. Keep your hands to yourself. Do those sound familiar? Have no fear, your awesomeness doesn't have to be questioned anymore! Make one of these weighted monsters to carry around with you, and your inner desire to touch, push and pull will be satisfied. Give your body the input it is crying for and please your adults at the same time!

## How to Make Ahead
Remove the label from your clean and empty laundry detergent bottle, then use the wiggly eyes, permanent markers and other materials to decorate your bottle to look like a monster. Don't worry, it can be a kind and silly monster if you want. It doesn't have to be spooky. Once you have your monster just how you want it, fill your bottle with a bag of uncooked rice.

## How to Use This Tool
If you are the type of kid that jumps through halls, runs in the grocery store or touches everything (including your friends) when you are in line, you will want to keep your buddy close by. Anytime you have to walk in a straight line or through an open space quietly and calmly, grab your buddy and carry him with you. The weight of the monster will slow you down, give input to your body and help you be successful!

## Challenge
There are tons of materials you can fill your buddy with. Try using dry beans, dried pasta, rocks, etc. Test which weight feels best in your hands and which material makes a walking buddy you can't live without.

## TRAIN YOUR ADULT ★

Active bodies are great, but sometimes we have to calm our active bodies enough to keep everyone safe and follow the rules of the building we are in. If you have an adult who is constantly barking at you to calm down in the halls, remind him or her that your proprioceptive (say: proh-pree-uh-sep-tiv) sense of body awareness is seeking input to tell you where you are in your space, and a weighted buddy will do the trick to keep you calm and centered.

## What You Need
Clean plastic laundry detergent bottle with its lid

Wiggly eyes

Permanent markers

Dry uncooked rice

# SECRET SHAPES

There are times when even the most elite secret agents can't use their sense of sight to solve a problem. While I don't expect you to go through your day blindfolded or fumbling through a deep, dark cave, you are constantly testing your visual (say: vizh-oo-uhl) sense without even realizing it. Think about how many times you tie your shoe without even looking down, or how you've learned to write your name without looking. That's because these lines and shapes are ingrained in your memory.

What if I told you that I could help you hone your secret-agent abilities by fine-tuning senses other than your sight. This game is perfect for training our brain to make connections with our tactile (say: tak-til) sense (just like we do when we write and button buttons). Soon, you'll be remembering spelling words, math facts and other tricky facts without a second thought.

## How to Use This Tool
This is a super simple game played anywhere. The first player turns his or her back to the second player. The second player then draws a shape on the forward-facing player with his or her finger. The player in the front has to guess what the other person drew.

You can draw basic shapes or get more creative and make pictures like rockets, lightning bolts, cat, dogs and robots. Your imagination is the key!

## Challenge
This is a great game to practice sight words, math problems and spelling words as well. Try to spell a word on your friend's back and see if he or she can tell what it is.

Younger superkids can match letters and numbers.

## TRAIN YOUR ADULT ★

Writing, drawing and recognizing letters and numbers takes a lot more than just your visual (say: vizh-oo-uhl) sense. By using all of your senses in this fun game, you are training your brain to use more than one of your super senses, so the next time you need to use one, they are that much stronger. While you might just be decoding shapes and pictures at first, you are working on fine-tuning your brain connections and muscle memory the whole time. This is a great game to train adults to use while you are waiting in line, sitting at dinnertime or even lying down for bed.

## What You Need
Your body

A friend and/or adult

# CHAPTER 5

# INCREDIBLE PLAY IDEAS THAT BOOST INDEPENDENCE AND FRIENDSHIP

Has an adult ever told you to just "go play"? If only it were that easy, right? Whether it's picking an activity to do or knowing how to get along with your friends when they want to play something you don't, "go play" can be hard for any superhero. Some of the best superkids around struggle with making friends, keeping friends and choosing activities (outside of saving the world). These activities and crafts will help you get your energy out, bust boredom and be the coolest kid on the block. From peaceful friendship hacks to ooey-gooey sensory experiences, these activities will boost your team player status, channel your inner energy and skyrocket your listening skills while having a blast each and every day.

WHAM!

CONFLICT RESOLUTION
★ SPINNER ★

Walk Away
and Let
it go

Talk it out

Use an "I"
(I FEEL) Message

Wait and
Cool Off

Apologize

Go to
another
activity

Ignore it

Ask them
to stop

Playtime should be full of fun, giggles and joy, but it often gets overrun with whining, tattling and arguing. Play is a funny thing because while grown-ups know how important it is for you to get outside, get messy and get your energy out, they forget that you don't always know what or how to play. The most important trick to making play full of joy and peaceful for everyone is to think outside the box. Think of unique ways to solve problems with your friends, play using all your senses and stretch your thinking using games. You'll have a whole toolbox of ideas for helping your grown-up support your out-of-the box ways! With a little bit of practice and patience, playtime can be exactly what it's meant to be: fun.

# STRAW ROCKETS

Have you ever felt tongue-tied, almost like you are speaking a foreign language? That, no matter your best efforts, your sounds and words are getting tied up at your lips and others struggle to understand you? This can be extremely frustrating for a rock-star kid like you. What you need is to boost your oral motor strength with some super fun games! These straw rockets are not only fun to make, but they will test your super strength.

## How to Make Ahead

Start by making the fins to your rocket. You will need to cut three triangles of equal size in your cardstock. One trick is to fold your paper into three parts so you can cut your triangles at the same time. Using any color craft tape, attach your fins to the bottom of your large smoothie straw. Next, cut the top of your smoothie straw so it is the same size as the regular bendable drinking straw above the bend.

Use your craft tape to cover the top of your large straw and finish decorating the rest of the straw to look like a rocket. Slide your smaller straw in the large straw and you are ready to launch.

## How to Use This Tool

Facing the rocket toward the sky, use your mouth on the small bendable part of the straw to blow as hard as you can to launch your rocket. This is a great calming activity or fun playful activity to do with your friends to hone your breathing skills.

## Challenge

How can you change your rocket to make it launch farther? Who can make their rocket go the highest? Which works better, a long or short straw?

## TRAIN YOUR ADULT ★

Just like other muscles in your body, you have to train your face muscles to be strong and flexible. When they are weak, it can lead to messy eating, trouble producing sounds for words and even delayed talking. Working the muscles in your mouth is easier than it sounds. In fact, every time you blow a whistle, suck a milkshake through a straw or blow bubbles, you are working those important muscles. This simple activity will enhance your vocabulary, help you increase the power and accuracy of your oral motor movements and even prepare you for handling your next big meltdown by teaching you to blow huge breaths.

## What You Need

Cardstock

Scissors

Crafting tape

Large smoothie straws

Regular bendable drinking straws

# ZOOMING CARDBOARD RACERS

**Superpowers**
coordination, balance, strength, teamwork, alertness, impulse control

**Sensory Systems**
touch, movement, body awareness

**Energy Scale**
⚡⚡⚡⚡⚡⚡

Blast out of this world with these awesome cardboard rocket racers! Are you one of those incredible kids who seems to have more energy than you know what to do with? The couch seems to call your name to jump on it, and running into things and people is your game? I get it. I do. One of the best ways to get that same intense contact is by pushing on something fun. These rocket races will have you zooming out of this world in no time!

## How to Make Ahead

Start by making sure the bottom of your box is secure by adding more packing tape along the seam and along the sides of the flaps. Next, use your box cutter to cut a rectangle out of one of the smaller side flaps to make the front window. Then cut a slant from the front of the box beside the window flap on each of the side flaps to make the sides and wings. Pull the flaps up to connect to the window flap and use your tape to connect the three sides. Attach the leftover triangles to the sides to make your wings. To make the front of your rocket, cut an extra box into two equal triangles and a large rectangle. Tape this on using your packing tape. Now, decorate your rocket using your aluminum foil, duct tape and markers or paint. Use your imagination. To add boosters, attach two disposable cups with crepe paper inside to the back of your box.

## How to Use This Tool

Take your rocket racers to a big hill or to an open area. Have your friends push you around or push around your friends. Try to race your friends for a fun and playful race full of pushing. If you are by yourself, you can fill your rocket with heavy items and push the rocket around your yard or house for the same great pressure and input.

## Challenge

This is just one way to make a rocket. Can you make a huge rocket to use as a calm-down spot in your home? What can you add to your rocket to make it move faster on the ground?

## What You Need

Large cardboard boxes

Packing tape

Box cutter (with adult help)

Aluminum foil

Duct tape

Markers and/or paint

2 disposable cups (optional)

Crepe paper (optional)

## TRAIN YOUR ADULT ★

When you are running, pushing and jumping, it is only natural for your grown-up to tell you to settle down. Especially if you are doing those things on their furniture. What you have is an underresponsive proprioceptive (say: proh-pree-uh-sep-tiv) system, which means you seek pushes and physical contact. To get the same satisfying movement and pressure as when you jump on the couch, try this terrific pushing game. Your adults will watch in awe as your overexcited body starts to release its energy and calm down before their eyes.

# POOL NOODLE OBSTACLE COURSE

**Superpowers**
motor planning,
coordination, balance,
strength, self-regulation,
following directions,
teamwork

**Sensory Systems**
movement, body
awareness, sight, touch

**Energy Scale**
⚡⚡⚡⚡⚡⚡⚡⚡⚡

Adventurers have to be quick on their feet and flexible in their thinking. Unfortunately, this quick thinking doesn't come naturally to all of us. This Pool Noodle Obstacle Course is perfect for training your brain to plan the movements your body makes, making you the quickest and smoothest athlete on the field. Your friends will love fine-tuning their coordination with this fun obstacle course. Shhhh! Don't tell them, but this actually helps them concentrate in school!

## How to Make Ahead

To make circles with your pool noodles, cut a cardboard tube lengthwise and roll it tightly. Put the roll in one end of the pool noodle and curve the other side of the noodle around to put the other end of the tube in the opposite end. While holding the ends together, use your duct tape to tape the connection closed. If you want to connect your circles, just tape them together on one side.

When you are setting up your obstacle course, place two chopsticks in the ground as stakes for your pool noodles. To make hurdles to jump over, place the chopsticks in the ground and then in both ends of the pool noodle so it makes an upside down *U*.

## How to Use This Tool

Once you have set up a fun obstacle course of different pool noodle arrangements, challenge your friends to go through it with you.

## Challenge

Be sure to add challenges to get you jumping, running, ducking, weaving and even crawling.

## What You Need

Pool noodles

Cardboard tubes

Duct tape (optional)

Chopsticks or wooden skewers

## TRAIN YOUR ADULT ★

Did you know your vestibular (say: ve-stib-yuh-ler) system is responsible for your movement and balance? In fact, some of the most adventurous people in this world crave this movement more than others. Tall buildings, jumping and spinning have nothing on these adventure seekers. If this sounds familiar, this is the activity for you! Another super cool fact is that all this twisting, turning, ducking and jumping will help you on and off the field. That's right, science tells us that increased movement increases our ability to focus on more challenging tasks. So train your grown-up to get you off the couch and outside running, turning and twisting.

# ICE BOWLING

Are you bored out of your wits? Can't think of anything cool to do with your friends? Set up a game of ice bowling and you will be the "coolest" kid on the block. Not only will boredom melt away, but your friends will love cooling off and letting off some steam with these icy bowling balls and DIY bowling pins.

## How to Make Ahead

To make your bowling pins, add food coloring to your bottles of water. We made each row of pins a different color, but you can do them all one color if you want. Next, prepare your bowling balls by filling several balloons with water and tying them off. Put them in the freezer overnight. Right before play, cut your balloon to remove your frozen bowling ball.

## How to Use This Tool

Set up your pins in a triangle just like bowling pins (one, two, three, four in each row). Stand back from your bowling pins and use your frozen bowling ball to try to knock down as many pins as you can before your bowling ball breaks into pieces or melts away.

## Challenge

You can add many things to your bowling pins (water, rice, beans, flour, rocks) to test your strength. Which materials make it easier to knock down?

To test your skills even further, try playing with a blindfold on.

## TRAIN YOUR ADULT ★

On a hot summer day, adults can be just as confused about what to do for fun as you sometimes are. Everyone runs out of ideas at some point, and this is the perfect cooling activity for you and your adults. It uses many of your senses, which will help you stay calm and centered the rest of the day. If you are a kid who can't stand loud noises, this is a much quieter version of the bowling alley.

## What You Need

10 water bottles (filled with water)

Food coloring

Balloons

Water

# CALMING SLIME

If you are a kid who loves getting his or her hands messy and ooey-gooey science, you will want to make a batch of this calming slime! I know, I know . . . slime does not seem like it could be calming at all, but I assure you, this slime will help you chill out, calm your nerves and get ready for any big adventure you and your friends have planned. This slime will have you using almost all your senses as you train your brain to slow down and squash your worries.

## How to Make Ahead

First, mix together equal parts glitter glue and water. One way to do this is to pour your glue into a bowl and fill your glue bottle with water or measure out precise amounts. Mix these together. If you want your slime even more glittery, now is the time to add more glitter. Add 1 to 2 drops of your favorite calming scent (like lavender or chamomile). Next, slowly add the liquid starch. You can add it by the tablespoon or you can slowly pour it. Stir your mixture until it starts to form a solid ball on your spoon or fork. To really get your slime good and mixed, you need to knead it and squeeze it with your hands. The more you squeeze it, the more it should feel like slime. If your slime seems too sticky, mix in a little more liquid starch and knead it some more. Store in an air-tight container and add water or liquid starch as needed.

## How to Use This Tool

Slime is perfect for rolling, kneading, dripping and oozing. It is fun to let it run through your fingers or ball it up tight and squeeze it. There are many ways to use your slime to help you calm your worries or big emotions.

## Challenge

Try hiding items like marbles or toys in your slime to "find." This is extra calming, as you have to focus on the items you are searching for.

## What You Need

½ cup (120 ml) glitter glue (any calming color)

½ cup (120 ml) water

Essential oil or scented extract (optional)

½ cup (120 ml) liquid starch

## TRAIN YOUR ADULT ★

Since this slime is extremely resistant and thick, it provides a great deal of deep pressure and joint compression. As you squeeze, fold, roll and even pull the slime, you are sending signals to your brain that are calming and organizing! While you twist, turn and roll the slime in your hands, your mind is almost immediately taken off guard. Train your grown-up to pull out this awesome slime when you are bouncing off the walls or starting to argue with your siblings. It will simmer down your energy or frustration, helping you get ready for calm indoor play.

# MIRROR, MIRROR EMOTIONS GAME

**Superpowers**
emotional awareness,
emotional regulation,
communication,
problem solving,
attention to detail, self-
awareness

**Sensory Systems**
sight

**Energy Scale**

Have you ever felt like your friends are a mystery? Do you struggle to read their faces when they are upset, happy, sad or even angry? This is not an easy task at all. In fact, emotional awareness is something that secret agents study for years. You have to notice the movement in the eyebrows, the direction of the eyes and even the slightest movements of the mouth. Have no fear . . . you too can train your inner feelings detective with this fun and engaging game of Mirror, Mirror.

## How to Use This Tool

This easy-to-play game is a great way learn your friends' emotions and the facial expressions that match their different moods. The first player starts by making a face that resembles an emotion they have (happy, sad, angry, surprised, etc.). Next, the other player tries to mirror or match the facial expression and body language of the first player. Pay close attention to the eyebrows, the shape of the eyes, the curl of the lips and open or closed mouths. Use the feelings list on page 182 to kick-start your ideas if you need to.

## What You Need
Your body
A friend

## Challenge

This game goes really well with the Feelings Masks on page 34. One player creates a face on the mask while the other player attempts to match the same facial expressions with his or her real face.

Try making this into a fun memory game by writing the emotions on index cards. As each player pulls a card, they have to show that emotion with their body and face while the other player guesses and matches the emotion.

## TRAIN YOUR ADULT ★

Noticing small changes on a person's face can open many doors of communication. However, when we misread these small changes on a grown-up's face, it can leave us feeling like our grown-up is angry, frustrated or disappointed in us. The next time you are unsure of how your adults are really feeling, simply ask them to describe their mood. Try getting your adults to play a game of Mirror, Mirror with you to familiarize yourselves with one another's facial expressions that match various feelings.

# SPACE INVADERS

## A Game of Personal Space

One of the hardest parts of being amazing and having super senses is that sometimes you don't even realize just how close you are getting to your friends. It's like they have a magnetic pull and you just can't seem to keep your hands off them or a safe distance from them. We have an invisible force field around us called personal space. This game will help you sense that invisible border and keep the perfect distance from both your friends and your foes.

## How to Use This Tool

Space Invaders is a good game to play at school or home. Players get a hula hoop to hold at their waist as their spaceship. There are a few ways to play this fun game.

**Stay Out of My Space:** Players walk around the space with their spaceship held at their waist. If a player touches anyone's ship (hula hoop), he or she must sit in the middle of his or her space on the ground. Speed up the play as time passes, making it harder to stay clear of each player's space.

**Space Tag:** One player is "It." This player is the only person allowed to run into someone else's spaceship. Players run in the space trying to avoid coming in contact with anyone else. If the person who is It touches a player's space, the player has to freeze in place until each player has been tagged.

## Challenge

Add streamers to the hula hoops to make it a game of Flag Tag. The player who is It has to remove the streamers without touching the person inside the hula hoop.

Use the hula hoops as spaceships when you have to sit for a long time. You can't move outside your hula hoop, but you can move as much as you need to inside your ship.

## TRAIN YOUR ADULT ★

Every superkid I have ever met has had an instance where they invaded someone else's space without knowing it. You see, your brain is still developing and learning what is too close and too far. Grown-ups can get really frustrated and misunderstand when you invade other people's space without asking (this could look like hitting, pushing or even sitting too close). If you find yourself struggling with a case of the space invasions, encourage your adult to play a game of Space Invaders with you or even give you a hula hoop to use as an out-of-this-world reminder.

---

**Superpowers**
impulse control, patience, teamwork, self-awareness, planning and prioritizing, self-monitoring, concentration, alertness, communication

**Sensory Systems**
movement, sight

**Energy Scale**

**What You Need**

Hula hoops

Friends

Large space

# SILLY SOUR VOLCANOES

Who says playing with your food isn't fun? These awesome volcanoes will have you opening your jaw in amazement! Just grab a few ingredients from your kitchen and you are ready to explore science with your senses! Plus, playing with your food will help you at your next mealtime when you are asked to try a new food!

## How to Make Ahead

With your adult's help, cut several lemons in half and place them in a tray. Add a pinch of baking soda to the top of the lemon and add a drop of dish soap on top. For added fun, add a few drops of food coloring to your lemon to see the reaction.

Use your Popsicle sticks to push on and mush your lemons until you get a fizzing volcano reaction.

## How to Use This Tool

This is a great sensory experiment to dig into when you have plenty of time on your hands. Try making a rainbow volcano by lining up six lemon halves and adding a color to each of the lemons. If you are the type of kid who loves to get messy and dirty, go right ahead and use your hands to squeeze the lemons to make your reactions. The more senses you use, the more you are connecting signals in your brain.

## Challenge

Try this experiment with other citrus fruits (grapefruit, orange, lime) and see if the reaction is the same. Do you like the smell of one fruit more than another?

You can also change the way your adult cuts the fruit. Try cutting a hole in the top or slicing it the other direction. Does it make a difference in the size of the reaction you get?

## What You Need

Lemons

Baking soda

Dish soap

Food coloring (optional)

Popsicle sticks

## TRAIN YOUR ADULT ★

This is the perfect activity to convince your adults to let you play with your food. Tell them it's science! Grown-ups love when you want to learn cool things, especially cool things that use your senses! Did you know that by trying experiments that use your senses, you actually become more familiar with the foods you try and more willing to try new foods? Doing an experiment that plays with your food like this one is the perfect introduction to sour foods and messy play all wrapped into one sweet experiment.

# DANCING OOBLECK

Rock stars need a good dance partner or back-up band. What if you could have both with this super oozy, super messy experiment? Using your auditory (say: aw-di-tawr-ee) sense of hearing and your tactile (say: tak-til) sense of touch, you will groove to the music while literally seeing the music move to the beat. Pull this out the next time your friends come over, and you will be the talk of the town. Who knows, maybe you will even win the next science fair with this one! It's a win-win.

## How to Make Ahead

Start by making a batch of oobleck by mixing the cornstarch and water until it is well mixed. Divide the oobleck into small bowls and mix in the food coloring of your choice in each bowl to make new colors.

After checking with your grown-ups to find the best subwoofer for the project, cover your subwoofer with plastic wrap and tape the plastic wrap down to keep it secure. Plug your subwoofer into an MP3 player with a test-tone track you can download for free online with your adults' permission.

## How to Use This Tool

Once you have everything mixed and your subwoofer is covered and hooked up, you are ready to go. Pour spoonfuls of your oobleck onto the middle of your speaker cone. Turn on the tone soundtrack and adjust the volume and tones until the oobleck begins to dance. You can use your spoon to get it started.

## Challenge

If you are the type of kid who is sensitive to loud noises, this is an activity that is good to use to determine the level at which noise starts to bother you. Be ready to stop early if the noise is too much.

Test different liquids on the speaker and explore which ones dance higher or faster.

## TRAIN YOUR ADULT ★

Noises are all around us. When we go to the grocery store, visit a restaurant or even walk down the street, we hear things. Some superkids have a supersonic auditory (say: aw-di-tawr-ee) sense of hearing and can hear things the rest of us mere mortals can't. This is a great activity to help you and your grown-ups learn your breaking points while having a lot of fun in the process. Train your adults to pay close attention to your likes and dislikes when it comes to messy hands and loud music. This activity is perfect for honing in on your sensory preferences.

### What You Need

2 cups (225 g) cornstarch

1 cup (240 ml) water

Food coloring

Old subwoofer or speaker

Plastic wrap

Tape

MP3 player

Spoon

# TIE-DYE TAG

A game of tag has never been so much fun! If you are a super sensory seeker, meaning you love to push and be pushed or touch and be touched, this is the game for you! Gather a group of your closest superhero allies for a rad game of Tie-Dye Tag. You will use nearly every one of your senses with this bright, bold and exciting game meant for the most active kids you know!

## How to Make Ahead

To make your tie-dye ammo, fill your water balloons with water and a few drops of tie-dye before tying them up. The more dye you use, the brighter the colors will be on your shirts.

## How to Use This Tool

In an open outside area, set out several tie-dye water balloons in buckets and have every player put on a white T-shirt. Each player uses one water balloon at a time to tag another player's T-shirt. Tag as many friends with your balloons as you can. There is only one rule you have to follow: You can tag only the T-shirt and nowhere else. If your balloon hits any other part of a player's body, you are out of the game.

## Challenge

If you don't like the feel of a wet shirt, no worries, you can still play this fun game by placing your shirt on the ground and throwing your balloons on your shirt. You will still get the fun of seeing the color splatter.

## TRAIN YOUR ADULT ★

Outside play is full of adventure and excitement, and sometimes our bodies turn into powerhouses of pushing and running into others. When adults see this energy, they are quick to shut a game down. This game will teach you and your friends about personal space while providing you with tons of sensory fun! Just remember, not all kids love all kinds of sensory input. Train your adults to be on the lookout for moods or behaviors that don't look like superkid fun. By realizing that not all kids play the same way, your adults will be armed with everything they need to help your play be as fun as it should be.

## Superpowers

motor planning, coordination, self-regulation. teamwork, following directions, self-monitoring

## Sensory Systems

touch, sight, body awareness, movement

## Energy Scale

⚡⚡⚡⚡⚡⚡⚡

## What You Need

Water balloons

Water

Tie-dye

White T-shirts for each player

# DIY GRAVITY SAND

Can you imagine what life would be like if you could defy gravity? Well, I can't exactly help you do that, but I can help you make some pretty radical sand that will amaze your friends and your grown-ups. This sand magically sticks together like playdough but stretches like slime when gravity pulls against it. It feels amazing to your tactile (say: tak-til) sense of touch and calms your mind and body with its magical powers.

## How to Make Ahead

In a small bowl mix the glue and water together until well blended. Next, add the liquid starch and stir until the mixture becomes slime. Pour your sand on a tray or in another small bowl, pinch off quarter-sized pieces of the slime and knead it into the sand. Continue to add more slime until your sand is the consistency you want (the more slime you add, the stretchier your Gravity Sand will be).

## How to Use This Tool

Gravity Sand is perfect to use just like playdough. It is moldable, bendable and rollable. It has the added property of gravity pulling it apart. Use this as a fun after-school activity or as a way to practice your facts to increase your memory. Build a sandcastle, make a cylinder and slice it with your finger, or create 3-D shapes that flow through your fingers. The options are endless.

## Challenge

Try using alphabet stamps in your sand to practice your sight words. After each word, simply flatten out your sand again to start over with a clean slate.

## What You Need

½ cup (120 ml) white glue

½ cup (120 ml) water

½ cup (120 ml) liquid starch

1 cup (365 g) colored fine sand

## TRAIN YOUR ADULT ★

I am pretty sure there is a secret pact among many grown-ups to avoid messy recipes. You see, instead of seeing an awesome calming activity, they see the cleanup afterward. You can ease their worries by promising to play in your designated area and help with the cleanup. A galactic tip is to put an inexpensive shower liner on the floor and contain your messy gravity sand in a plastic tub. Grown-ups don't realize how much some super kids crave the feeling of sand or slime on their hands. If you are a messy kid looking for fun, this is for you. Don't worry, once your adults see how calming this Gravity Sand is, they will want to mix up a truckload for you!

# STICKY SELF-PORTRAITS

Do you have a secret identity that sometimes fools even you? Maybe some days you don't even recognize your own feelings or emotions. Recognizing your own feelings and emotions, also known as self-awareness (say: self uh-wair-nis), takes a lot of practice and isn't a task that comes naturally to most superkids. The truth is, even adults misinterpret your facial expressions and responses. This sticky sensory art will get you in touch with your feelings and help you describe your own emotions to the adults in your life.

## How to Make Ahead

Start by cutting your tissue paper into small squares and set them to the side for later. On the nonsticky side of the contact paper, draw the outline of your face and details such as your eyes, mouth, nose and even eyebrows with your permanent marker. Next, tape the large square of contact paper on a window with the sticky side facing toward you. Carefully pull off the backing on the contact paper so you can see the sticky side you will use when you are ready to make your self-portrait.

## How to Use This Tool

Next, use your various colors of tissue paper to fill in the color of your face. For example, use red for your lips, blue for your eyes and colors that match your skin color and hair color. If you need to add more details after you have finished using the sticky part of the contact paper, use a small amount of glue to apply outlines and small pieces of tissue on top of the base. Finally, use another large piece of contact paper with the sticky side facing away from you to cover your art and protect it.

## Challenge

Try to make a few self-portraits that show your moods. This way you can have a visual display of your emotions to help you communicate with your adults and friends.

This is a great activity for superkids who hate getting their fingers messy but want to try a fun art activity.

## What You Need

Tissue paper (various colors)

Scissors

Clear contact paper

Tape

Black permanent marker

Glue (optional)

## TRAIN YOUR ADULT ★

Not only are Sticky Self-Portraits a great boredom buster (which adults love), but they can be perfect for bridging the communication gap between you and your adults. Sometimes adults struggle to find the words and ways to talk to you about your behaviors and emotions. This is a great activity for your grown-up to use to sneak in those confidence-boosting compliments as he or she works with you to create an awesome self-portrait.

# WALK THE LINE

## Tape on the Floor Games

Just because running away to the circus isn't an option for you, that doesn't mean you can't pretend to be a tightrope walker and channel your inner daredevil with these balance-boosting games. Put your finger to your nose and follow the trail, but don't dare step off the track! Not only will these games put your feet on track and test your balance, but they will harness your brain's ability to focus using your visual and vestibular senses. Are you too quick on your feet and adults always tell you to slow down? This is the activity for you!

## How to Make Ahead

With your adult's permission, clear an area on your floor or outside on the sidewalk where you can make your lines. Next, use your tape to make various line shapes on the ground. You can make straight lines, zigzag lines, curved lines or even lines that make shapes and letters.

## How to Use This Tool

There are so many awesome ways to use the tape once you have made your lines. Here are some of our favorites.

**Balance Beam**: Pretend your lines are balance beams or tightropes and try to walk on your tiptoes all the way down your line without stepping off.

**Jump the Line**: Another fun game is to make several lines in a row (almost like the lines on a ladder). See how many lines you can jump over without tiring out.

**Car Tracks**: Curved lines and zigzags are really fun for getting down on the floor on your stomach and using them as a road for your toy cars. Remember, don't let the cars fall off the road.

**Pom-Pom Racers**: Get down on your belly with a friend and challenge them to a race with straws and pom-poms. Use your straw to blow your pom-pom along the lines until you reach the end.

**Maze Moves**: Use your tape to make a maze on the floor with twists and turns. Challenge your friends or family to solve the maze you made for them.

## Challenge

Think outside the box for new ways to use your tape to increase your balance and coordination. Can you make a city, tic-tac-toe or even an obstacle course?

## TRAIN YOUR ADULT ★

Some superkids simply have more energy than their grown-ups know how to harness. When your body gets proprioceptive (say: proh-pree-uh-sep-tiv) input in your joints and bones from jumping and moving, your brain gets signals that calm your body and your mind (which is what every adult is looking for). The opposite is just as true. If you get sluggish and sleepy during schoolwork or homework, this is the perfect boost you need to wake up your brain!

**Superpowers**
coordination, balance, focus, concentration, strength, alertness, self-regulation

**Sensory Systems**
movement, body awareness, sight, touch

**Energy Scale**

**What You Need**
Painter's tape or craft tape
Open space
Toy cars (optional)
Straws (optional)
Pom-poms (optional)

# UPCYCLED SUPERKIDS CAPE AND MASK

**Superpowers**
self-confidence, hand strength, planning and prioritizing, following directions

**Sensory Systems**
touch, sight

**Energy Scale**

What would a superkid do without his or her own cape and mask? Everyone knows superheroes need these important tools to keep their secret identity and become the greatest form of themselves. While you are already your best self, these simple upcycled capes and masks will have you transforming into your super self in no time at all and spreading the awesomeness with your friends! No sewing or special patterns required!

## How to Make Ahead

To make the cape, start by laying your T-shirt on a large piece of cardboard to protect the surface underneath. Use a ruler or yardstick to trace a straight line from the outside of the neck of the shirt to the bottom corner of the shirt. Do this on both sides of the neck so you have a triangle shape left. Carefully cut along the lines and around the neck of the T-shirt. Now you have an awesome cape. If you want to make it adjustable, cut the neck in the front and add Velcro to the ends.

To make the mask, on the leftover piece of T-shirt or felt, draw a mask outline with a permanent marker. Cut your design out and use a hole punch to create holes on both sides of the mask. Next, measure elastic string the size of your head and tie the string through the holes.

## Challenge

Use leftover felt or another shirt to cut shapes (like stars and lightning bolts) to add to your cape using the glue. You can even cut out the first letter of your name to personalize your cape.

## TRAIN YOUR ADULT ★

Sometimes the behaviors of a superkid can get in the way of the true superpowers hiding behind the cape and mask! If you feel like your grown-ups have lost sight of your superpowers, have a chat with them, let them know how you are feeling and come up with a plan together to highlight those skills that might be hiding behind the big emotions and behaviors you are still learning to tame.

## What You Need

An old T-shirt

Cutting mat or large piece of cardboard

Ruler or yardstick

Scissors

Velcro

Felt (optional)

Permanent marker

Hole punch

Elastic string

Glue (optional)

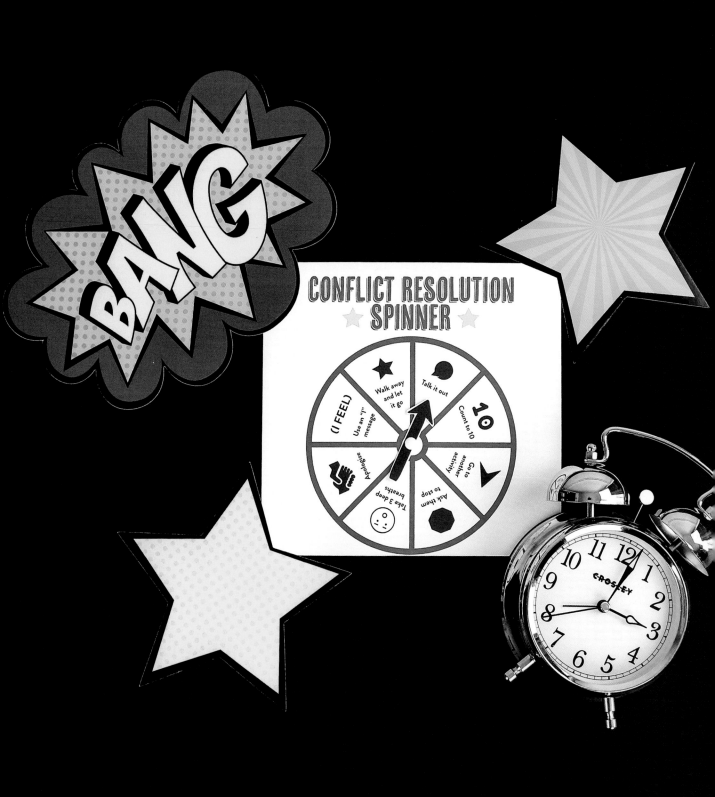

# CONFLICT RESOLUTION SPINNER

**Superpowers**
self-regulation, communication, problem solving, emotional regulation, risk taking, flexible thinking

**Sensory Systems**
sight

**Energy Scale**
⚡⚡

It never seems to fail. You get together with a bunch of your best super pals, everything seems to be going smooth and then *bam*, a huge argument erupts. While it is bound to happen between all super pals at one time or another, it doesn't make it any more fun. Knowing how to react and respond in the middle of a battle can be critical in keeping your friendships safe and healthy. This Conflict Resolution Spinner will help you remember positive choices you can make at the first sign of trouble!

## How to Make Ahead

Start by copying or tearing out the Conflict Resolution Spinner on page 197. Cut along the dotted lines to cut out the wheel and the spinner. Using a brad fastener, attach the spinner to the middle of the wheel. If you want to keep your wheel safe and make it long lasting, cover both sides with clear tape or contact paper and trim the edges.

## How to Use This Tool

Sometimes in the heat of the moment our brains freeze up. This is what grown-ups call the fight, flight or freeze response. While this is completely normal, it doesn't help you solve your problems with your best buds.

The next time you are frustrated or feel a swarm of emotions coming on during playtime with your friends or siblings, spin your wheel of choices to find the perfect solution. This chart will help you keep your cool and your friends at the same time.

## Challenge

Don't like the choices we picked for you? That is completely fine. Use the blank wheel on page 198 to pick your own choices.

## What You Need

Conflict Resolution Spinner (page 197)

Scissors

Brad fastener

Clear tape or contact paper (optional)

## TRAIN YOUR ADULT ★

Grown-ups love the words *calm down*. What they don't realize is that calming down isn't as easy as those two words. In the heat of the moment, your brain needs a little help picking the right actions so you don't scream, kick or say something you don't mean. Practicing the alternatives on this wheel will set you up for success with both your friends and grown-ups. Ask them to role-play a few frustrating scenes with you so you can choose better when you are upset.

# CHAPTER 6

# MAXIN' AND RELAXIN' NIGHTTIME RITUALS FOR A PERFECT END TO YOUR DAY

Bedtime, shmedtime. Don't adults know that superheroes do all their best work when everyone else sleeps? No wonder you never want to wind down and go to bed. Unfortunately, as growing superheroes, you need your rest more than adults do. While winding down, taking a bath and getting ready for another great day sound like boring tasks, trust me . . . they will boost you to the next level!

From bubbling bath play to calming retreats, these activities will help you ground your energy, rest your mind and soothe your worries for a better night's rest so you can prepare your body for another action-packed day.

SUPERKID
TIP

From the moment you get home from school until the time you close your eyes at night, you are pulled in about ten thousand different directions. Do your homework, eat your dinner, take your bath, play with your sister, get ready for bed, go to sleep . . . With the laundry list of activities that get fit into your nighttime routine, it's no wonder this time of day can be such a gigantic headache for both you and your grown-ups. The secret to a smooth and peaceful evening rests in your attitude. You have the choice to let the stress and worries build up and get you down or to fight off those evil mood-altering villains and relax into the evening. When you start to feel the worries of the world settling on your shoulders, I want you to take a step back, make a decision to have a good attitude and risk trying new strategies to remain calm, cool and collected.

# CRASH LANDING

## Stuffed Animal Crash Pad

Not all adults will let you jump on the bed before bedtime. So what is an active superhero to do when he or she has pent-up energy and the desire to crash and bounce? Make a super-duper crash-landing pad, that's what! The only place you will want to crash after this is into your pillow for a good night's rest!

**Superpowers**
emotional regulation, strength, motor planning, alertness, impulse control, organization

**Sensory Systems**
body awareness, movement, touch

**Energy Scale**

## How to Make Ahead
This crash pad is simple to set up. Lay your duvet cover flat on the floor in an open area (your bedroom, the living room, basement, etc). Fill your cover with all of your stuffed animals. The goal is to get your duvet cover filled to the brim with stuffies. Button or zip up your duvet cover and you are ready to go!

## How to Use This Tool
Your crash pad is perfect for crashing, smashing, jumping, falling and pushing into. When you feel tons of energy that you need to let out or you are feeling pent up, head over to the crash pad for 10 to 20 minutes of safe pouncing fun.

## What You Need
Twin-size duvet cover

All your stuffed animals

## Challenge
Don't have many stuffed animals? It's okay. Visit your local upholstery shop and ask for sofa stuffing remnants to use instead.

### TRAIN YOUR ADULT ★

Taming wild animals should be added to every adult's job description. Let's face it, sometimes you are just as wild as the animals at the zoo and have tons of energy to get out. One of the easiest ways to calm even your wildest roars is to spend a few minutes playing on this crash pad in the evenings at the beginning of your nighttime routine. It gives you a place to get your final pushes and input to your proprioceptive (say: proh-pree-uh-sep-tiv) sense of body awareness. When your adults see how peacefully you sleep, they will have you using the crash pad every day!

# DRAGON BUBBLES

**Superpowers**
emotional regulation, self-regulation, self-calming, impulse control, self-awareness

**Sensory Systems**
oral, touch, sight

**Energy Scale**
ᗘ ᗘ ᗘ

No matter how awesome your day was, your inner dragon can still be ramped up and overcharged, leading to some pretty fiery meltdowns before bedtime. Since taking deep breaths doesn't come naturally to all kids, practice is what we need. These dragon bubbles are the perfect way to practice letting out all the air from your lungs and releasing your frustrations.

## How to Make Ahead

After removing the label and cleaning your bottle, have an adult help cut the bottom of the bottle off with a box cutter. Next, cut the toe off your sock and cover the new opening and secure with a rubber band. Measure and cut your green paper to the length of your bottle and wrap the bottle with the paper. Secure with glue or hot glue with adult supervision. Cut out two small long rows of spikes, folding in the bottoms, and glue them along the top side of the water bottle. Next, glue two green pom-poms behind these spikes near the mouth of the bottle (these will be the eyes). Finally glue a wiggly eye on each pom-pom.

## How to Use This Tool

There are two ways to play with your new dragon bubble maker.

**Dry Dragon Bubbles:** Anytime you are starting to get frustrated or nervous or have trouble with your big feelings, take three big dragon breaths by blowing into the mouth of your bottle. Nothing will come out the other side, but the calming effects will still be there.

**Fire Breathing Dragon Bubbles:** When you have time outside, set out a shallow dish and add water and dish soap. Mix these together and dip your dragon into the solution (sock-side down). Place a few drops of food coloring on your sock for added fiery effects. Now, blow as hard as you can! You should see the fire billow from the dragon's mouth.

## TRAIN YOUR ADULT ★

One of the hardest parts about being a super kid is having super emotions. Grown-ups can be doing everything right, but your brain is still developing and you are still learning how to control your dragon rages, so they need to help you remain calm. These Dragon Bubbles are the perfect way to practice big breathing before the explosions begin. This simple craft will train your brain to take the deep breaths you need when you are upset. With every big breath, you will add oxygen to your brain, quickly filling you with radical calming chemicals.

## What You Need

Clean and dry plastic bottle (standard water bottle is the perfect size)

Box cutter (with adult help)

Old yellow sock

Rubber band

Green cardstock paper

Glue

Large green pom-poms

Wiggly eyes

Shallow dish or pie tin

1 cup (240 ml) water

2 tbsp (30 ml) dish soap

Red, yellow and orange food coloring

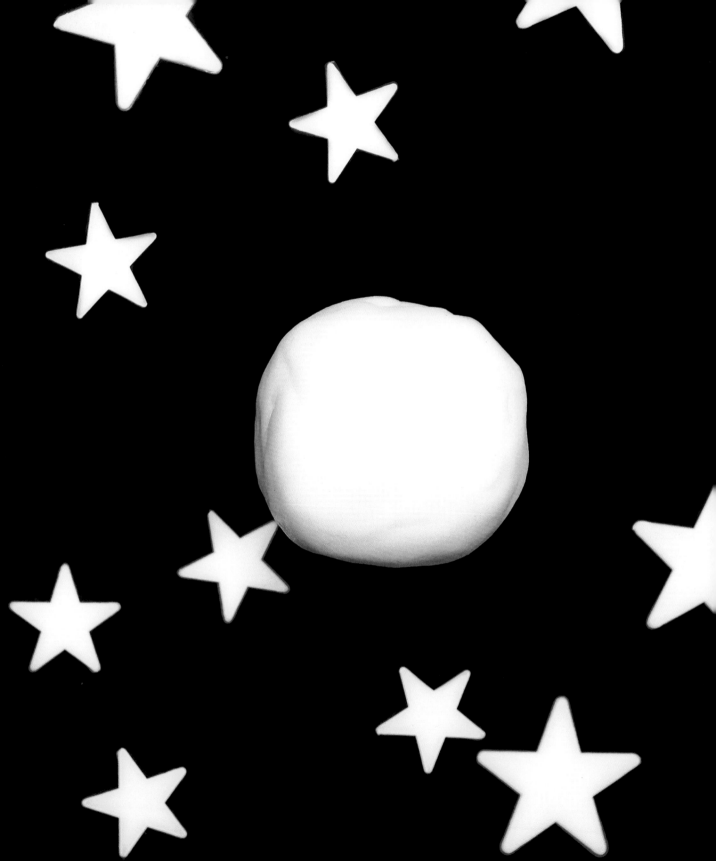

# GLOW IN THE DARK PLAYDOUGH

Some of the biggest villains we face at bedtime are our stress and worries. Our mind seems to think of all the things we still have to do, a test the next day, an upcoming field trip . . . you name it, your mind thinks it. After dinner one night, whip up a batch of this Glow in the Dark Playdough and watch your big worries get smashed away.

## How to Make Ahead
In a bowl, mix the petroleum jelly and the cornstarch until the dough is silky and smooth. Once the ingredients are mixed together well, set the dough out in the light so it can "charge."

## How to Use This Tool
When you are ready to enjoy some calming playdough time, grab your black light and dough and turn off the lights. With the black light on the table where you are playing, you should be able to see your dough glow while molding your dough into any shape or form you wish.

## Challenge
Use the 2-Ingredient Focus Dough on page 106 and make a hole in the center of the dough. Add 1 tablespoon (15 ml) nontoxic glow in the dark paint and knead until mixed in for another version of glowing dough.

For even more calming effects, add a few drops of lavender essential oil to your dough during the mixing process.

## TRAIN YOUR ADULT ★

Adults might not think of playing as a way to help you calm down before bedtime. In fact, they might think you are trying a new stalling tactic. Just remind them that playdough lets you work out your frustrations, stresses and worries through your fingertips. The science is in the dough. When you press, knead and roll the dough through your fingertips, your tactile (say: tak-til) sense of touch sends calming signals, a.k.a. endorphins, to your brain that will ensure a peaceful night's rest.

## What You Need
½ cup (120 ml) petroleum jelly

2 cups (225 g) cornstarch

Black light

## Optional
2-Ingredient Focus Dough (page 106)

1 tbsp (15 ml) glow in the dark paint

Lavender essential oil

# TIGHT SQUEEZE BURRITO ROLLS

**Superpowers**
self-regulation, emotional regulation, focus, self-awareness, teamwork, impulse control

**Sensory Systems**
touch, body awareness

**Energy Scale**
⚡⚡

Does your body wiggle and move constantly? Does "settle down" seem like an impossible demand from your adults? It sounds like you need to be squeezed! Grab your favorite blanket and your adult and get ready for a silly, calming game of Tight Squeeze Burrito Rolls. Your adult will be amazed at just how much this calms you and gets your body ready for the rest of the night.

## How to Use This Tool
Lay your favorite blanket flat on the floor and lie down along one edge to become the filling of the "burrito." Make sure your head is out of the blanket completely and your hands are at your sides. Next, have your adult roll you up inside the blanket until the entire blanket is wrapped tightly around you, just like a burrito. Finally, have your adult add the "toppings" by squeezing your shoulders, elbows, hips, knees, etc. and telling you what burrito toppings they are adding next.

Make sure you tell your adult what you like and don't like about the squeezes, and only stay in the blanket a few minutes at a time.

## Challenge
Burritos aren't the only thing that roll up. Pretend to make hot dogs, sushi rolls, banana splits and more. Let your imagination be your guide for connecting with your adults in a calming way.

## TRAIN YOUR ADULT ★

Have you ever begged your adult to tuck you in tight at night because it makes you feel safe and secure? This is why this activity is so effective in calming you down. Don't get tucked in only at bedtime. Science tells us that adding deep pressure over a large area of our body can send calming waves through our nervous system. The effect is a relaxing sense of order and weightlessness. Nervous about going to a new place? Do a wrap before you leave. Busy and bouncing before school? Try a burrito roll-up. Once your adults learn this new trick and see how calming it is, they are going to thank you over and over. They will wonder why they didn't try this sooner!

## What You Need
Large blanket
Your adult

# INTERGALACTIC BATH BOMBS

Destroy the bedtime blues and defeat any intergalactic space alien with these fizzing bath bombs. Whisk away to a place of calmness and peacefulness while turning your bath into a galaxy of fizzes and sparkles. This bath bomb will have you begging to take your next bath!

## How to Make Ahead

Start by mixing together your dry ingredients in one bowl. It's a good idea to get everything mixed as evenly as you can. Slowly mix in the water and oils, but be careful not to overmix (this will cause the fizzing to start early). Separate your mixture into small bowls and add a few drops of food coloring to make blue, purple and pink mixtures.

Next, scoop 1 teaspoon (5 g) of each color mixture into a soap mold or form in your hands. Make a small ball with layered colors to look like the galaxy. Set your bath bombs to the side to dry for at least 2 hours.

## How to Use This Tool

The next time you dread the nighttime bath, get out an Intergalactic Bath Bomb and add it to your bathwater. Watch the water turn colors and the bubbles start to happen. You won't be able to resist such a soothing and inviting bath.

## Challenge

This recipe works with any color combination to make bath bombs. Try making rainbow colors, superhero colors or your favorite color.

Try making your bath bombs into different shapes by using candy molds. The sky is the limit to the shape and sizes you can make.

## TRAIN YOUR ADULT ★

Bath time is a dreaded time of day for most grown-ups. They fear the arguments, the screams and the naked bodies running through the hall. Show your adults baths can be fun and even relaxing if they just take the time to find out what bothers you so much about baths. Does the water bother your skin? Do you fight the fact that *bath* means *bedtime*? Being open and communicating with your adult about what you don't like about bath time will leave both of you happy and hopefully clean. Also, if you struggle to calm your body for bedtime, a bath can do just the trick by adding deep pressure and sensory input to your entire body and giving you one last chance to move, twist and turn to get all your energy out before you lay your head on your pillow.

## What You Need

1 cup (206 g) baking soda

½ cup (115 g) citric acid (can be found at the grocery store)

½ cup (56 g) cornstarch

½ cup (122 g) Epsom salts

1 tsp (5 ml) water

Essential oils (optional)

2 tbsp (30 ml) almond oil

Blue, purple, pink food coloring

Soap mold (optional)

# MAGIC MOOD-CHANGING BLANKETS

Being a kid is a lot of work. Being a superkid is downright exhausting. It can leave you with a cranky attitude, even if all you want to do is be happy! We've talked about how adding pressure and weight to your body can trick your brain into releasing calming chemicals that will actually improve your mood. This weighted blanket is easy and fun to make and will have your adults wanting one of their own when they see the change in your mood from your good night's rest!

## How to Make Ahead

First, get your bags ready. Start by laying out your resealable plastic bags into five rows (across), with five bags in each row. Evenly divide your rice into all twenty-five bags. We used 2 cups (370 g) in every bag. Roll your bags until all the air is pushed out and seal the bags. Lay each bag of rice flat and use a ruler to line your bags in straight rows with the bags 2 inches (5 cm) apart on the sides and between the rows.

To tape your bags together, place a long strip of duct tape along the top of the resealable plastic bags across the entire row. Carefully turn over your row and tape the other side. Do this for all five rows. Next, lay all of your rows flat and begin taping between the rows. Be sure to cover the bottom of the top resealable plastic bag and the top of the next row's bags. Do one row at a time, front and back, before going to the next row. Next, tape the columns (up and down) together using the same method. Finally, cover both sides of the entire surface with a layer of duct tape.

To make the blanket cover, lay your fleece fabric on a flat surface and fold it in half. Cut along the fold (it doesn't have to be a perfect line). Keep both pieces of fabric together. On each corner, cut out a 4-inch (10-cm) square. To make the fringe, lay your ruler next to the cut corner and cut into both pieces of fabric 5 inches (13 cm) to make slits in the fabric. Do this on all sides of the fabric. Start on one corner of the blanket and begin tying the pair of slits together just like you would tie a balloon or your shoelace. Do this on three of your sides.

To complete your blanket, carefully slide your taped rice bags into the pocket you made with your fabric. Next, tie the final fringe together along the fourth side of your fleece. There is no need to secure your taped bags to the fabric, because it is perfectly nestled in your fabric just the way it is. Your blanket is warm and ready to go.

## How to Use This Tool

This blanket is great for getting to sleep, calming down after school or wrapping over your shoulders when you start to get nervous.

TIP: Your weighted blanket should be 10 percent of your weight. So, if you weigh 50 pounds (23 kg), this is the perfect weight for you. If you weigh more or less, change the amount of rice you add to your blanket accordingly.

## TRAIN YOUR ADULT ★

This might be one of the most time-consuming projects in the book, but I can assure you it is the one with the most benefits. Much like other weighted tools (see the Weighted Snake Lap Buddies on page 93 and Tight Squeeze Burrito Roll on page 165), weighted blankets are used to apply deep pressure to a large area of your body and give your proprioceptive (say: proh-pree-uh-sep-tiv) sense of body awareness the push back it needs to calm your brain for a good night's rest. The science is pretty cool too. When your body receives this deep pressure, your brain releases serotonin (say: ser-uh-toh-nin), a mood-stabilizing chemical that plays a huge role in sleep. When you use your blanket at night, your serotonin naturally converts to melatonin (say: mel-uh-toh-nin), a natural hormone used by your body to regulate your sleep patterns, which gives your body a signal to take a rest. Store-bought blankets like these can be very expensive. This DIY no-sew version is the perfect way to get your adults on board to help you calm and relax.

## What You Need

25 quart-size (24-L) resealable plastic bags

5-lb (2.25-kg) bag uncooked rice

Ruler

Duct tape

3 yd (2.7 m) fleece fabric

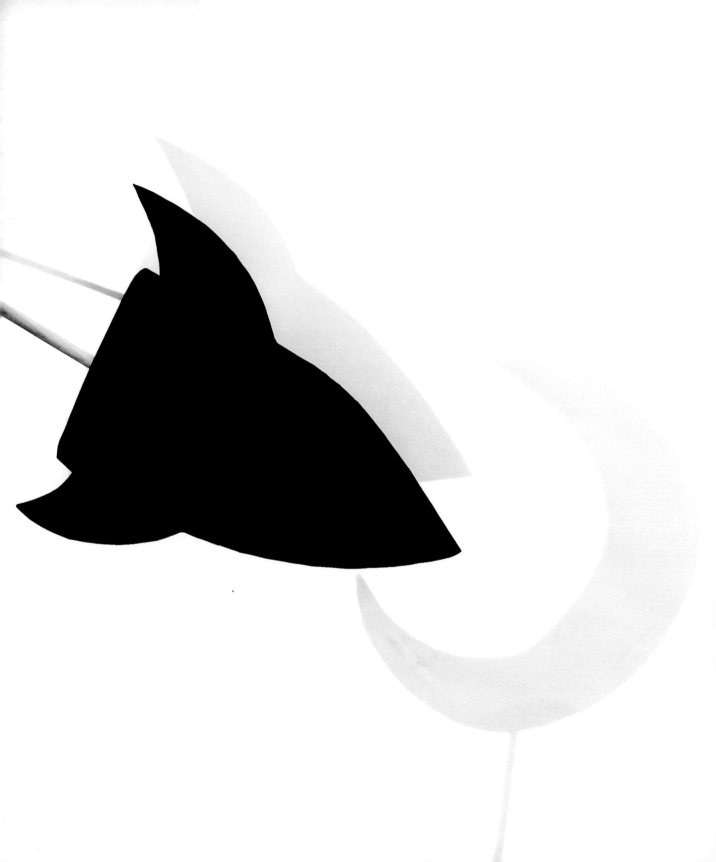

# OUT OF THIS WORLD SHADOW PUPPETS

**Superpowers**
attention to detail, problem solving, self-awareness, communication

**Sensory Systems**
sight, touch

**Energy Scale**
⚡⚡

Have you ever noticed that some of your biggest adventures happen when the lights get turned out? Suddenly your dresser becomes a big hairy monster and your curtains become a looming ghost waiting to spook you. Every adventurer knows that this is just his or her imagination playing tricks, but that doesn't always stop the worries from being big and hairy themselves. Simple shadow puppets will train your brain to recognize shadows and changes in light so you can rest assured your room is a safe place to sleep.

## How to Make Ahead
On your cardstock, draw and cut out a large rocket (similar to the countdown schedule on page 89). On other papers, draw and cut out various-size stars. Finally, draw and cut out a crescent shape for the moon.

Use tape to attach your drawings to a wooden skewer or chopstick.

## How to Use This Tool
Shadows can be very scary things, but not if you understand the science behind them. During the day, grab your puppets and your flashlights and turn off the lights. Hold your flashlight behind your puppet facing the wall and see the shadow it creates on the wall. Notice how the shadow changes when you move your flashlight closer and farther away.

## Challenge
After playing with your rockets and space puppets, try testing other things in your room to see what shadows they make. What shadow does your coat hook make? What happens when you shine light toward your big stuffed animal in the corner?

## What You Need
Cardstock paper

Marker

Scissors

Tape

Wooden skewers or chopsticks

Flashlights

### TRAIN YOUR ADULT ★

When superkids get scared, it confuses grown-ups. They might even tell you, "It's no big deal" or, "There's nothing to worry about." This doesn't mean they don't care; it just means they don't see what you are worried about and can't tell how important it is to you. If strange shadows are something keeping you up at night and you struggle to get your adult to understand, try this fun activity during the day to get them on board and explore this concept in a nonthreatening way.

# ADVENTURER'S RETREAT

**Superpowers**
emotional regulation, self-regulation, alertness, self-monitoring, balance, self-calming

**Sensory Systems**
movement, body awareness, touch

**Energy Scale**
⚡⚡

Big adventures can lead to big emotions and feeling overwhelmed. It is very common for your senses to get overwhelmed and go into retreat mode. If you aren't careful, this overstimulation of your senses could send you spiraling into a meltdown that could leave you and your adults speechless. One of the easiest ways to recenter your body and remove yourself from as much sensory input as possible is to build a simple retreat. This free-hanging retreat is the perfect balance between calming and soothing. Grab a book and hide away until you calm down!

## How to Make Ahead

Have your adult wrap your sheet under a table and tie the sheet in a double knot on the top of the table. It should look just like a hammock. It is important to have an adult's help so you can keep this activity as safe as possible.

## How to Use This Tool

This retreat makes the perfect spot to hang out in after dinner or before bedtime. Grab your pillows and stuffed animals and cuddle up for a quiet place away from the rest of the noise of the family.

## What You Need

Queen-size linen sheet or woven baby wrap

Kitchen table

Pillows (optional)

Stuffed animals (optional)

## TIPS ★

Test the knot before climbing into your retreat.

Remove the retreat when no one is using it to keep everyone as safe as possible.

Tie your sheet so that you are not too high off the ground and can easily get in and out of the hammock.

## TRAIN YOUR ADULT ★

Not only will this retreat give you your own personal space to retreat to, but it will calm your vestibular (say: ve-stib-yuh-ler) sense of movement, leaving you in a peaceful mood. Your grown-up probably remembers rocking you as a baby to calm you down. This retreat is no different. Use the retreat right before bedtime for a bonus calming effect, since rocking back and forth will help settle your developing brain into a restful peace.

# DIY RAINBOW SENSORY RUG

Are you a kid that loves the feeling of grass between his or her toes? Tiptoe over the rainbow with this super sensory-filled rug that will fulfill all your tactile urges to touch and feel everything before bedtime. Make this colorful and cheery rug so the last thing your feet hit before bed tingles your senses and brightens your mood.

## How to Make Ahead

To make the pom-poms, lay the end of the yarn over the palm of your hand and wrap the yarn around your hand one hundred times (give or take) and cut the yarn. With the yarn still wrapped around your hand and your palm facing you, thread another piece of yarn behind the bundle of yarn and tie a knot around the yarn. Carefully slide the bundle off your hand and tie the extra piece on the opposite side of the bundle, leaving a long tail from this extra piece. Finally, cut the middle of all your loops on both ends and fluff up your pom-pom. Make eight of these for every color.

Once you have all your pom-poms made, make the rug. Lay your no-slip mat on a flat surface and tie a red pom-pom around two of the holes in the non-slip mat, starting in the corner. Attach the rest of your red pom-poms in a straight line. Start each new color as a new row and attach the pom-poms the same way as the first pom-pom. When all of your pom-poms are attached, turn your rug over and trim all the tails left over and any mat still showing.

TIP: I know it looks like a time-consuming project, but I promise this will be finished before you realize and will be worth every minute. Try setting goals and getting through each section or through a certain number of pom-poms each day until you finish. It took us 15 minutes after school for about 2 weeks.

## How to Use This Tool

Place this rug in your room at the foot of your bed or next to your safe and calm place in your home. When you are feeling the need to calm your emotions or energy, run your toes or fingers through the rug to send calming signals to your brain.

## Challenge

You can make this rug with any color combination or design. Simply tie your pom-poms in a different pattern or order. Try using only your favorite colors or a fun pattern that you would find calming.

## TRAIN YOUR ADULT ★

Normally, your grown-ups might see a project like this and just think it's a waste of time, especially if they can get the store-bought version without all the work. What if you could tell them that a project like this will strengthen your hand muscles, which will make you more successful in school (hello, good penmanship), and it will calm you as you fidget with the pom-poms? The next time your grown-up sends you to your room, you will be happy to comply, knowing you have this awesome rug to run your fingers and toes through. Not only is the end result perfect for calming your senses (and your attitude), but creating the project is just as magical and rewarding!

**Superpowers**
attention to detail, hand strength, emotional regulation, alertness, self-calming

**Sensory Systems**
touch, sight

**Energy Scale**
⚡ ⚡

## What You Need

Yarn (red, orange, yellow, green, blue, purple)

No-slip rug mat

# WORRIES AWAY BASKETBALL

No superhero should end his or her night with a head full of worries. It is proven science that having a head full of big worries and thoughts can keep you from getting the sleep you need to be at your best every day. Getting those thoughts and worries out doesn't have to be a struggle anymore, with this active game that not only gets out your negative thoughts but also gets out your last traces of energy so you can lay your head on your pillow and prepare for another awesome day tomorrow!

## How to Make Ahead

Any basket will do for this activity, but if you really want to tell your worries to take a hike, you can make a simple "worries away" basket to throw your worries in at the end of each night. Use stickers or permanent markers to decorate your basket with something that will remind you that your worries are getting trashed so they can't bother you anymore.

Cut a few pieces of paper (any color) into fourths to make small rectangles. Keep a stack of papers and a pencil near your bed to write down your biggest worries of the day.

## How to Use This Tool

As part of your bedtime routine, write down your biggest worries of the day on a piece of paper. This can be anything from an upcoming holiday to worries about someone's health. No worry is too big or too small to jot down.

Now for the fun part. Crumble up that worry into a ball and try to shoot it into your "worries away" basket. Don't stress if you miss the basket, just shoot until you get all your worries in the trash and your mind is clear.

## Challenge

If you can't write your worries down, don't stress. Just draw pictures. Remember, this is a no-worries zone. Don't add to your distress. Just do your best.

## What You Need

Clean, unused trash can

Stickers (optional)

Small pieces of paper

Pencil

## TRAIN YOUR ADULT ★

"Don't worry" just doesn't cut it when there is something stuck in your brain. Your grown-ups aren't trying to dismiss your cares and struggles, believe me. They just don't realize how sticky these thoughts might be for you. Help them help you get these thoughts unstuck and thrown away by sharing your basket with them. Science has proven that writing about your worries works! It frees your brain and opens up space for more useful thoughts. In your case, this means you will have room to dream of your next adventure and be ready to focus tomorrow when you wake up with a fresh, clear mind!

# FAIRY TALE SLEEPY TIME ICE POPS

**Superpowers**
emotional regulation,
self-calming,
communication, planning
and prioritizing

**Sensory Systems**
taste

**Energy Scale**

All princes and princesses must end their day at some time despite how much fun they are having. Unfortunately, sometimes our brains don't get the message it's time to shut down, and we get insomnia (say: in-som-nee-uh), the inability to fall asleep. While it might sound like a dream come true to stay up forever, insomnia can actually make you pretty grumpy and keep you from being your best self. For those times you just can't fall asleep, you need a little boost. These sleepy time ice pops will send any prince or princess to dreamland for a restful night's sleep. Plus, they taste super yummy and give you an excuse to have dessert before bedtime!

## How to Make Ahead
Put all the ingredients into a blender and blend until everything is mixed evenly and smooth. Pour your mixture into ice pop molds and place in your freezer overnight. When it is time to enjoy the ice pops, simply pull one out and enjoy!

## How to Use This Tool
Just before bed, enjoy one of these sleepy-time ice pops and watch your yawns start to flow.

## Challenge
While you are eating your ice pop, talk about your day with your adults. This is a great way to clear your mind and get ready for a peaceful night's sleep.

### TRAIN YOUR ADULT ★

When you start to burn the midnight oil and refuse to go to sleep, adults assume you are doing this to defy their rules. I know that couldn't be further from the truth. Superkids have active brains and busy bodies that don't always shut down naturally like adults think they should. Let your brain chemistry do the work for you with these healthy, sleep-inducing ice pops. Glycine, which is found naturally in gelatin, decreases your big worries and promotes mental calmness, while the potassium in the bananas is a natural muscle relaxer. Together, the gelatin, strawberries and bananas are a super sleepy time treat that can't be beat. Just watch out: Your adults might sneak a few on their restless nights.

## What You Need
½ cup (120 ml) orange juice

½ cup (120 ml) soy milk

1 banana

½ cup (125 g) strawberries (fresh or frozen)

3-4 tbsp (45-60 g) yogurt

1 (4-oz [113-g]) packet gelatin

# THE SUPERKIDS ⚡ ENERGIZED ACTIVITY GUIDE

This book is full of activities that can either boost your energy or bring you down a notch and ground you back on Earth. This guide is your go-to reference for finding the just-right activity to bring your body back to the just-right level of energy so you can rock your day.

## Energy-Taming Activities

# THE SUPERKIDS FEELINGS REFERENCE GUIDE

Let's face it. Superkids have many more emotions than just "happy" and "sad." Learning to name, recognize and regulate those emotions is the key to a killer day! This is your guide to the most common emotions you encounter on a daily basis.

- Angry
- Annoyed
- Anxious
- Bored
- Brave
- Calm
- Confused
- Curious
- Depressed
- Determined
- Disappointed
- Distracted
- Embarrassed
- Excited
- Exhausted
- Frustrated
- Furious
- Guilty
- Happy
- Hurt
- Jealous
- Lonely
- Lost
- Loving
- Overwhelmed
- Proud
- Relaxed
- Sad
- Scared
- Shy
- Sick
- Silly
- Thankful
- Tired
- Uncomfortable
- Worried

# TOOLS TO CONQUER EVERY DAY

Having an awesome day every day isn't an easy task. What you need is a toolbox full of all kinds of things to help you get through any hurdles you might face on your daily adventures—books, websites, toys, tools, exercises and more. I've gathered a huge list of resources on my site so you and the grown-ups who love you can rock each and every day with ease.

Head over to www.superkidsguide.com to find totally terrific links to things like:

- Visual schedules and charts to help you organize your day
- Rock-star brain breaks and exercise videos to get you moving
- Sensational tools to fulfill your need for movement, wiggling and even chewing
- Inspirational YouTube channels to remind you just how awesome you really are
- Spectacular sensory-rich play ideas to keep you busy, busy, busy
- Totally cool book lists that will help you understand why you do the things you do
- And so much more . . .

# SUPERKIDS TEMPLATES ⚡

Just like the most powerful superheroes need an escape plan and the most famous rock stars need a song list, you need visuals to help you conquer your biggest obstacles. In this section, you will find the pages to help you through the hardest parts of your day. Since they are ready to go, you can cut them out or copy them so you can use them again and again . . . I've even made it so you can make your very own designs to rock your day. Several templates have a "blank" side so you can customize it to your own superpowers. The choice is yours.

From rocking morning routines to a choice wheel to help you in sticky situations, these visual tools will help you stay organized, confident and in a good mood all day long!

# MY MORNING ROUTINE

## TO DO          DONE

 Get Clean

 Bathe

 Brush Teeth

 Brush Hair

Clothes in Hamper

 Get Dressed

 Shirt

 Pants

 Socks

Shoes

 Eat Breakfast

 Wash Hands

 Prepare Food

 Eat

 Clean Up Dishes

 Get Ready for School

 Put Things in Backpack

 Pack Lunch

 Put on Jacket

 Turn Out Lights

# ⚡ MY ROUTINE ⚡

| TO DO | DONE |
|---|---|
| ◯ ◯ | ◯ ◯ ◯ |
| ◯ ◯ | ◯ ◯ ◯ |
| ◯ ◯ | ◯ ◯ ◯ |
| ◯ ◯ | ◯ ◯ ◯ |

# MY LUNCH CHOICES

VEGGIE

FRUIT

PROTEIN

DRINK

SNACKS

SWEETS

OTHER

# MY _____ CHOICES

_____ PICK ____

_____ PICK ____

_____ PICK ____

_____ PICK ____

_____ PICK ____

_____ PICK ____

_____ PICK____

# ★ THINGS I PACK EVERY DAY ★

GLASSES

LUNCHBOX

BOOKS

HOMEWORK

PENCILS

FOLDERS

JACKET

WATER BOTTLE

# ⚡ WHAT'S NEXT? ⚡

| Hang Backpack | Eat Snack | Read Book | Brain Break | Do Homework | Clean Up Supplies |
|---|---|---|---|---|---|
| DONE! | DONE! | DONE! | DONE! | DONE! | DONE! |

| Pick Up Toys | Make Bed | Help With Dishes | Take Out Trash | Put Away Laundry | Help Sweep |
|---|---|---|---|---|---|
| DONE! | DONE! | DONE! | DONE! | DONE! | DONE! |

# FEELINGS BOOKMARKS

## WHEN I FEEL ANGRY I CAN,

Take 3 deep breaths

---

**BAM!**

Close my eyes

---

**ZAP!**

Get a drink of water

---

**KA-BOOM!**

Squeeze my hands

---

Take a walk

## WHEN I FEEL SAD I CAN,

Get a hug

---

Squeeze a pillow

---

Rub a blanket

---

Draw it out

---

Play with Playdough

# FEELINGS BOOKMARKS

WHEN
I FEEL _____ I CAN,

Pow! Pow!

BAM!

ZAP!

KA-BOOM!

Pow!

WHEN
I FEEL _____ I CAN,

BOOM!

BAM!

ZAP!

POW!

SMASH!

# CONFLICT RESOLUTION
## ★ SPINNER ★

# CONFLICT RESOLUTION ★ SPINNER ★

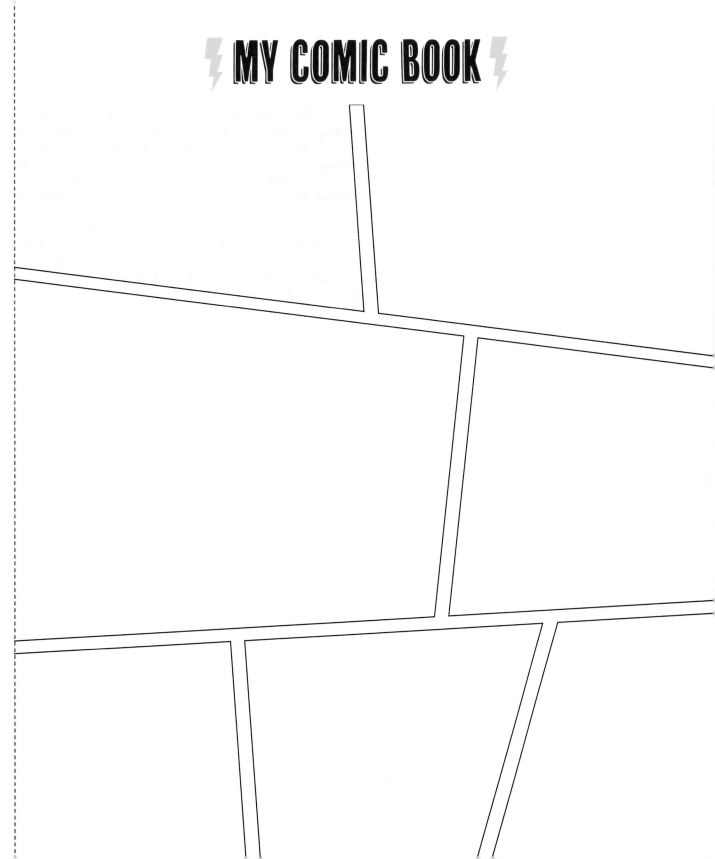

# MY COMIC BOOK

# ACKNOWLEDGMENTS

Being a superkid doesn't happen on your own. In fact, I bet if you took a minute to think of everyone and everything that goes into your having super wonderful days, you would run out of fingers to count everyone on. If you tried to be spectacular every day on your own, you would fizzle out quickly.

Just as you need a team of family, friends, teachers and secret supporters to be successful, I need a super team to be the best grown-up sidekick I can be.

You've just finished reading a book with tips, strategies and tools to help you teach the grown-ups who love you how to help you conquer every day. Did you know that this book would not be in existence if it wasn't for my amazing team backing me up? That's right, even grown-ups need help to be successful, and this is the page of the book where I am going to brag on all the people who helped me make this book possible so you know you aren't the only one who needs a team.

A huge thanks goes to the team at Page Street Publishing. They are the super-secret headquarters that is in charge of making this book happen. Without the entire team, we wouldn't have everything from the tremendous title to the actual book you are holding in your hands.

I believe all kids are superkids, but I have to admit I am a little biased toward my own three: Flora, Caiden and Elijah. They endured countless trials of play recipes, endless days of "mom working" and ridiculous amounts of takeout food while we worked together on this book. In truth, they are my inspiration. If my kids didn't have their own unique likes and dislikes and hadn't been misunderstood by other adults, I might never have thought to write a book for kids just like them. Thank you for pushing me to be a better mom for you!

My husband, Jason, was the ultimate rock star by listening to me brainstorm endlessly, giving me a push when everything felt too hard to finish and taking care of our little superkids so I could write for you.

(continued)

# ACKNOWLEDGMENTS (CONT.)

I owe the entire idea of this book to my good friend, Karen, who has been the best cheerleader I could ever wish for. Thankfully, I had a killer team of friends cheering me on and supporting me through the entire process. There are too many to list without boring you, but I have to brag on a few. Jess, Ewa, Amanda, Kelly, Rachel, Lauren, Sarah, Colleen, Anne, Vanessa, Jackie and Kaylene—I couldn't have done this without you! You rock!

Just like you have your own unique strengths, I have things I am good at and things that I am not as good at. That's why I called in my super troupe to help with some of the details of the book. Some of the awesome recipes, like Marvelously Moody Pizzas and Fairy Tale Sleepy Time Ice Pops couldn't have happened without my talented photographer friend, Jennifer Tammy. All of the ridiculously cool printables in the back of this book were all created by the very talented Brittany Mays. Thank you both for making this book shine!

Take another flip through the book. Did you notice all the smiling faces and truly amazing superkids? These kids are true superheroes! Did you know some of them actually waited out thunderstorms to take these pictures! Thank you so much to all of the kids and their parents for being willing to try my crazy ideas, all in the name of fun! Conner, Henry, Olivia, Abby, AJ, Katherine, Sirius, Vivienne, Simon, Owen and Freddie—never quit being totally awesome!

So many of the activities in this book were inspired by great authors, teachers and bloggers. I have to thank Tammy from www.housingaforest.com for the inspiration for the Dancing Oobleck on page 143 and my friends Claire and Lauren at www.theinspiredtreehouse.com for inspiring me to share the magical world of sensory superpowers with the world.

If you are reading all these words thinking you'd like to write a book someday, know that you can do anything you put your mind to! I am forever grateful for my dear friend Amanda for answering a stranger's email a few years ago encouraging her to start a blog. Thank you to all the blog readers at Lemon Lime Adventures over the years, the members of our private support group and everyone who has believed in me and encouraged me over the years.

Finally, no book would be complete without you, the reader! You are important to this story, just like you are for every book you will read for the rest of your life. Without you, there would be no book, no story to tell and no adults to train. Thank you from my entire team for reading this book and believing in yourself. You are a superkid. Don't let anyone ever tell you different.

# ABOUT THE AUTHOR

Dayna Abraham is the mother to three totally awesome superkids who inspire her every day to be the best grown-up sidekick they could ask for. When she's not helping her kids conquer the world, she keeps busy by blogging at www.lemonlimeadventures.com, writing books like *Sensory Processing 101*, *STEAM Kids* and *The Unofficial Guide to Learning with LEGO®* and drinking lots of coffee. She loves getting her hands messy and creating crazy science projects and crafts to keep her superkids busy at home. Before she was a writer, she was a National Board Certified teacher, where she met some of the coolest superkids on Earth. As a little girl, she wished grown-ups and other kids saw her as a superkid, so now she's made it her mission to inspire kids like you to love who they are and embrace their differences.

# INDEX